# SECRE_
# PRACTICE

Mary Bosticco was born in Britain, brought up in Italy, and has since pursued a varied career in Europe and America as well as the UK. She began as a multi-lingual secretary in Buenos Aires, then moved into the fields of journalism, management consultancy, public relations and authorship.

She is now a full-time writer, and the author of several successful books on management techniques and secretarial practice, including *Top Secretary*.

## TEACH YOURSELF BOOKS

# SECRETARIAL PRACTICE

## Mary Bosticco

*Advisory Editor: Gladys G. Skinner*
*Lecturer in Business Studies*
*South Nottinghamshire College of Further Education*

TEACH YOURSELF BOOKS

Hodder and Stoughton

**To Pearl, my wonderful sister-in-law
and a secretary supreme**

*First published 1984
Second impression 1987*

British Library Cataloguing in Publication Data

Bosticco, Mary
Secretarial practice. – (Teach yourself books)
1. Secretaries     2. Office practice
I. Title
651.3'741        HF5547.5

ISBN 0 340 35262 0

*Printed and bound in Great Britain for
Hodder and Stoughton Educational,
a division of Hodder and Stoughton Ltd,
Mill Road, Dunton Green, Sevenoaks, Kent,
by Hazell Watson and Viney Ltd,
Aylesbury, Buckinghamshire
Photoset by Rowland Phototypesetting Ltd
Bury St Edmunds, Suffolk
This volume is available in the USA from:
Random House, Inc.,
201 East 50th Street, New York, NY 10022*

# Contents

## Acknowledgments

It would be remiss of me to send this tome on its way without formally thanking those individuals, companies and organisations who helped me in its preparation. I am most grateful to them for lightening my burden.

I should like to thank the Royal Society of Arts, Pitmans College and the London Chamber of Commerce and Industry for permission to reproduce past examination papers, and the following for supplying photographs or other material: British Telecom, Mita Copystar, Pitney Bowes, Roneo Alcatel, Sperry Univac, Expandex Ltd, Cumbermay Ltd, and Wiggins Teape.

My grateful thanks are also due to Philip Edwards, Jack Evans, Michael Gray, Phoebe Read, J. T. Jew, Carole Larking and David Walters. I am also indebted to Barclays Bank, and especially to V. Webber and G. M. Jarvis; to the Post Office; to MAC-Management Consultants, and to Racal Electronics. Finally, I am most grateful to Patricia Curtis, the Reference Librarian at Maidenhead Library, for her cheerful and unstinting cooperation.

# Preface

This book aims to inform and assist all those who are interested in a secretarial career – either by starting at the bottom of the ladder, or by returning to it after an absence of some years. Offices have changed considerably in recent years, and automation has changed and continues to change a secretary's work, bringing new challenges, new opportunities and also new threats, of which she must be aware if she is to tackle them and surmount them.

For those readers wishing to go on to more formal studies this book introduces all the topics required by the following courses:

Pitman, Secretarial Practice Intermediate;
London Chamber of Commerce and Industry, Private
    Secretary's Diploma;
Royal Society of Arts, Secretarial Duties II;
BTEC National, Secretarial Services

As well as the technical side of the job, this book deals with the less tangible aspects of a secretary's work – the things, in fact, which make all the difference between being an upgraded shorthand-typist and a true secretary.

As we all know, women now occupy many executive positions, from first-line supervision to chief executive. It follows that the 'chief' so often mentioned in this book could just as easily be female as male. I have not, however, felt justified in distorting the English language by writing 'he/she', 'his/her', and so on, but I have none the less specifically mentioned the feminine gender where it is appropriate to do so.

It might be as well to mention that some secretaries are male, and indeed in some Middle Eastern countries all secretaries are male. I can assure them that they too have been borne in mind all the time, even though this may not be always apparent.

In preparing this work, I have been able to draw on my experience on both sides of the desk, as secretary and executive, not only in Britain, but in several other countries.

Mary Bosticco

# 1

# The Big Picture

In one respect at least, a secretary is the most fortunate of workers, for there is hardly an organisation, whether public or private, which does not employ a secretary. The vista which opens before you, then, is broad indeed.

## The various organisations

First of all there are the two great divisions: the public sector and the private sector. This simply distinguishes the organisations which are funded by the government – that is to say, paid for from the public purse – and those funded by private capital.

The public sector comprises central government itself; local government, such as the county and district councils; the public corporations, such as the Post Office and British Rail, and many other bodies.

The private sector comprises the following:

### 1   The sole trader
He finances and runs his own business, and so makes all the decisions, takes all the profits, suffers the losses and does a great deal of the work himself.

### 2   The partnership
If the sole trader's business flourishes, he often finds he can no longer cope on his own, and takes a partner to share the burden of providing the capital and running expenses, as well as the

other responsibilities of the business. Professional people such as doctors, solicitors, accountants and estate agents frequently set up partnerships.

### 3   The co-operatives
These comprise the Co-operative Wholesale Society (CWS), which manufactures and imports goods, and the Retail Co-operative Societies, which purchase these goods from the CWS for sale at retail prices to their customers. The retail co-operatives are owned by their members and anyone over sixteen who is willing to buy a share, usually costing £1 or £2, can apply for membership. The CWS is, in turn, owned and controlled by the retail co-operative societies.

In recent years a number of worker co-operatives has been set up in Britain. They are owned and controlled by the workers. Many of these enterprises were taken over by the workers when the original owners failed and wanted to close down the business. While not all the worker co-operatives have been able to make a go of it, some have been outstandingly successful and, according to a report recently presented to Parliament, this type of enterprise is very much on the increase.

### 4   The company
This is the most common type of business enterprise. Basically, there are two types of company: public and private. Both are financed by, and therefore owned by, their shareholders, who, by putting money into the company, quite literally buy a share – or several shares – of the capital of the business. If it prospers and makes a profit, some of this is distributed to the shareholders at the rate of so much per share. This share of profit is called a *dividend*.

The shareholders appoint a board of directors to make the important company decisions and to run it along the lines laid down by its Memorandum and Articles of Association. These documents stipulate the company's objectives and the rules for its administration, respectively.

## What they do

All business enterprises exist for one or more of three purposes: (*a*) to manufacture goods, (*b*) to buy and sell goods, or (*c*) to provide a service to the public. Ford and ICI are examples of manufacturing companies. Department stores and the small shops run by the sole traders are examples of businesses engaged in buying and selling, that is to say, in trade or commerce. They buy goods at wholesale prices and sell them to the customers at retail prices.

A hairdressing salon is an example of a business providing a service. Other examples are solicitors, architects and dentists. These last three, however, being professionals, often do not think of themselves as being in business, but as running a 'practice'.

While the three broad divisions are quite valid, it is as well to bear in mind that every business enterprise should aim to provide a service to its customers: the manufacturer producing the goods that people need, at prices they can afford; the trader selling the goods people need, again at prices they can afford; and the professionals and service industries likewise serving the needs of their clients. All of them should give good value for money. Obviously, every business also has to make a profit, otherwise it could not endure for long.

## How they are run

### The public sector
**Central government**   The work of central government in Britain is done by two groups of people: those elected for a limited period, and the permanent officials, known as civil servants. The government is divided into Departments of State, each responsible for a certain field and headed by a Minister. These ministers make the major decisions, while the civil servants on their staff carry out the day-to-day running of the department, and provide their employers with the information they need to tackle the problems which arise. The work of the departments is coordinated by the Cabinet – a Government committee of senior ministers, appointed and chaired by the Prime Minister.

**Local government**   As with central government, two groups of people are involved in the running of county, district and borough councils, as well as city corporations. The first group consists of elected councillors, and the second of the officers and staff who are employed by the authorities.

Councillors are usually elected for three or four years. They carry out much of their work through committees, which deal with such matters as housing, health and education. The committees are responsible to the council as a whole and must report to it periodically. Decisions must not only be in line with the Council's general policy, but also must be reached democratically after discussions which may sometimes be protracted or even acrimonious. The public and Press have the right to attend Council meetings, as well as some committee meetings.

Each authority is organised into a number of departments, headed by a chief officer. The chief executive acts as coordinator, leading and motivating the team, and liaising with the councillors.

**Public corporations**    These are business enterprises set up by Act of Parliament and financed by the Government. The Government also lays down their policies and appoints a Board to take care of the everyday running of the enterprise. An example is the National Coal Board (NCB).

**The private sector**
In the private sector, the sole trader finances and runs his own business according to his own capabilities and requirements. With a partnership the situation is very similar, the only difference being that as there are two or more partners – with a limit of twenty in the case of a professional practice – there has to be a little more formality. In other words, the partners should agree among themselves as to their rights, liabilities and duties. If they are wise, they will draw up a deed and put all the details of their agreement in writing.

Companies and co-operative societies are run in a similar way. The shareholders of a company appoint a Board of Directors to formulate policy and broadly steer the company in the right direction; in retail co-operatives it is the members who appoint a board, which in turn elects a chairman and appoints managers for the day-to-day running of the business.

A company board of directors may consist of some *executive directors*, who form the company's top management team, and some *outside directors*, who may be controlling shareholders or people with influence and useful contacts.

The *managing director* is the chief executive director and has the authority to carry out the policies agreed by the board. The board is responsible for the nature of the policies, and the managing director for putting them into practice.

The *company secretary* has the statutory responsibility for preparing the accounts and seeing that certain returns are filed with the Registrar of Companies.

## The chain of command

Fig. 1.1 shows a typical organisation chart, in this case of an imaginary company which manufactures goods and also sells them to retail shops with the aid of a team of salesmen. At the top, and really outside the chart, is the Board of Directors. The first individual in the chart, at the apex of the pyramid, is the managing director. He guides and inspires the whole operation. His style and example percolate all the way down the organisation, and in fact no company can be better than its managing director.

Under the managing director, and directly responsible to him in this organisation are four executives: the *marketing director*, the *production director*, the *financial comptroller* and the *personnel director*. These are the four executive directors on the board. They are responsible, respectively, for everything to do with selling the merchandise, in the broadest sense of the word; for producing the goods; for taking care of the financial aspects; and, finally, for company personnel. They form the top management team.

These four executives have three or four other departments under them, with their respective heads, known as *middle managers*. Under them are one to four other departments or sections, whose heads are known as *first-line supervisors*. At the foot of the pyramid are the 'foot soldiers': the salesmen on the left, the factory workers in the centre, and the office workers on the right.

Not all the smaller sections of the company are indicated in the chart, but it shows quite clearly how the company is organised into departments. Every company employee, from managing director to filing clerk, is responsible to his immediate superior and no one else, but while typists, salesmen and factory workers are responsible only for their own work, a department head is responsible for the work of the whole department.

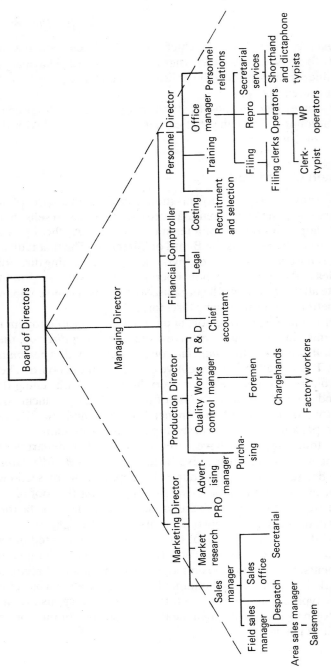

**Fig. 1.1** An organisation chart

Those executives who are responsible for the main functions of the business, such as manufacturing or selling, are known as *line executives*. Each of these has authority only over his own subordinates. Other departments are not directly responsible for the main operations of the business, but provide a supporting service to the line management. A word processing centre is a good example of a supporting service. Executives in charge of such servicing departments are known as *staff executives*. Line managers are, in effect, their customers.

Fig 1.1 shows that the personnel director has an office manager reporting to him. This particular executive is responsible for three sections: Secretarial Services, Reprography, and Filing. This shows that the company has centralised its office functions. In another company each department might keep its own files, have its own typists and shorthand-typists, and give its reprographic work to an outside firm. In other words, its office services may be departmentalised. These two ways of handling office services greatly affect a secretary's job and the main differences will be described in subsequent chapters in this book.

The organisation chart in Fig. 1.1 is known as a pyramid chart and this form of organisation has been followed for as long as workers have been organised into large groups. It is as well to bear in mind, however, that this structure is being challenged and some companies have adopted other forms of organisation. Even within the pyramid type, there are as many forms of business organisation as there are trading policies, and the one shown in Fig. 1.1 is only one example.

## What's in it for you?

For you, one of the most interesting aspects of the organisation chart is the fact that secretaries are usually employed at every level, and in most departments. This means not only that many jobs are potentially available, but that a business enterprise offers an enormous variety of fields in which to work. In fact, the organisation chart could be used as an illustration of a possible career path for you, and there is no reason why, in your supporting role, you should not work your way right to the top of the pyramid.

Suppose, however, that you begin work with our hypothetical

company. You might start as a shorthand-typist in the secretarial services section, and then you might become a junior secretary to the office manager. Later, you might get a more senior secretarial post with the personnel director. By then you may have decided that you rather like personnel work, and you could gradually work your way into that field. Alternatively, if you are very good at your job, you could one day become secretary to the managing director, and move on to become his personal assistant.

This is the conventional way up. No new career paths have yet emerged, although the new technology has produced some new jobs for experienced secretaries with word processing experience. The main ones are word processing supervisor/coordinator, trainer and customer support representative.

## The information system

If you look once again at the organisation chart in Fig. 1.1, you might wonder how all these departments keep in touch. How do they coordinate their work? How do they liaise with customers and suppliers? How does the billing department know that a salesman has sold a dozen chairs or sideboards and when they should bill the customer for them? How also does the customer know that his order has been despatched?

The answer is twofold. First of all, connections are maintained by letters, internal memoranda, Telex, the telephone, paging systems – a whole range of information devices which are described in Chapter 5. Secondly, information is passed on using commercial documents which have worldwide application and are designed to transmit data in the simplest, quickest and most practical way. As a secretary you will probably not get involved with all of these documents, but it is none the less useful for you to know what they are. So here are some of the most common, in alphabetical order:

*Bill of exchange* This is a written order addressed by A to B, signed by A and requiring B to pay a specified sum of money on a certain date.
*Bill of lading* This is a document issued by a shipping company detailing the goods shipped on behalf of an exporter, the destination, the names of the vessel and owner, and all other pertinent details.

*Certificate of origin* This is a document indicating the country in which the goods have been manufactured. It enables the importing country to levy the correct tariff.

*Consignment note* This accompanies goods transported by outside carriers and includes delivery instructions.

*Credit note* This notifies a customer that his debt, as invoiced, is being reduced by a stated amount. This can happen because goods have been found faulty, short, or as a result of an error on the invoice. Credit notes are usually typed or printed in red.

*Customs declaration* This is a list made out by an exporter, detailing the goods he is sending abroad and their value. It enables the customs authorities in the receiving country to levy the correct duty from the purchaser.

*Debit note* This is the opposite of a credit note and advises the customers that an additional amount is due. A debit note may have to be sent out if a mistake has been made in the original invoice.

*Estimate* This gives details of a job to be done, or service to be rendered, together with relevant cost, sent out in response to an inquiry. As the word implies, the cost is intended as a guide only (see also Quotation).

*Inquiry* A request for details of goods offered for sale.

*Invoice* A commercial invoice sets out full details of goods despatched and shows what the customer owes (see Fig. 1.2).

*Letter of credit* A document opened by an importer transferring funds to a bank abroad. The bank then settles the exporter's account on the importer's behalf upon presentation of documents proving that the goods ordered have actually been despatched.

*Order* As the name implies, this is quite simply a formal order for goods. A customer uses either his own printed order forms or a form provided by the supplier. Sales representatives usually carry an order form book to facilitate the writing out of their customers' orders.

*Overdue account letters* Sometimes called reminder letters, these are standard letters sent to customers who have not settled their accounts.

*Packing list* Also known as a delivery note or despatch note, this is a list of the goods despatched. It is enclosed with the goods and enables the customer, or his warehouseman, to check off each item as he unpacks it and to make sure the order is complete.

## INVOICE

The Successful Manufacturing Co Plc,
46, The Rye,
High Wycombe,
Buckinghamshire. SL8 5TY.
Telephone: High Wycombe 23420
Telex: 949322
Vat Registration No. 328 1494 87

To:

The Happy Retail Group Plc
25 Sunny Road
LONDON
WC1 5XY

Transaction:  SALE

| | | |
|---|---|---|
| Your Order No. | 2611 | |
| Invoice No. | 158 | |
| Invoice date | 20.11.8- | |
| Tax point | 20.11.8- | |
| Delivery date | 20.11.8- | |

| Style No | Quantity | Description | Unit price £ | Total cost £ p | VAT Rate | VAT £ p |
|---|---|---|---|---|---|---|
| HW25 | 100 | Occasional chairs | 20.00 | 2 000.00 | | |
| YW30 | 50 | Coffee tables | 15.00 | 750.00 | | |
| XW50 | 50 | Telephone tidies | 12.50 | 625.00 | | |
| | | | | 3 375.00 | | |
| | | Trade discount @ 50% | | 1 687.50 | | |
| | | Total Goods | | 1 687.50 | 15% | 506.25 |
| | | VAT 15% of £3 375 | | 506.25 | | |
| | | | | 2 193.75 | | |
| | | E&OE | | | | |

Terms: Net

**Fig. 1.2**   A commercial invoice

The 50% discount allows a percentage of overheads and a margin of profit to be added before selling at retail. 15% is charged for VAT (Value Added Tax), which is a sales tax, on some goods only, at varying rates. It is levied at every trading stage, and can be reclaimed at the end of the accounting period. Traders with a turnover of less than £18 000 pa are not liable for VAT.

*Proforma invoice*   This is a document giving full details of goods being offered, for the purpose of quotation. It is used mainly in the import/export business. The proforma invoice enables the importer abroad to apply for all the documents he needs to import the goods and to open a letter of credit. Prices in these documents are usually given as (*a*) CIF (Cost Insurance Freight) followed by the name of the port of destination, which means that the price covers the cost of the goods, the insurance and freight (or transport) to that port; (*b*) C&F, which covers cost of the goods and freight only, with the insurance cost indicated separately; or (*c*) FOB (Free on Board) at a stated port of embarkation, which means that the cost of delivery to the ship and loading on board are included, but not the cost of insurance and freight to the importing country.

A proforma invoice can also be used in other circumstances, for example if a supplier is dealing with a customer for the first time and wants to be paid before the goods are despatched. In this case the proforma amounts to a request for payment. A proforma invoice can also be used if no payment at all is required, for instance if a faulty item is being replaced free of charge.

*Quotation*   A detailed offer of goods, in response to an inquiry. In the export business it usually takes the form of a proforma invoice.

*Receipt*   This is an acknowledgement of payment. Statements of account and invoices are frequently stamped 'Received with Thanks', signed and dated, and returned to the customer. Nowadays, however, receipts are usually issued only if a customer specifically asks for one, as a cheque is accepted as evidence of payment and receipt.

*Service agreement*   This is a contract under which a supplier undertakes to maintain equipment supplied for a stated period after sale or through a period of hire.

*Statement of account*   Sent out monthly by the accounts department, this details the customer's transactions over the month and shows the total sum due, or the balance if in credit. Customers are expected to settle any outstanding debts on receipt of the statement.

Some of the documents listed contain much the same information. For instance, a packing list (or delivery note) is similar to a consignment note and both are very much like an invoice, the only difference being that neither of the first two requires a price to be shown. In order to save time and effort, therefore, many companies have sets of documents pre-printed and headed 'Invoice', 'Packing List', etc., with all but the last being carbon backed. In this way it is possible to produce four or five different documents in one typing operation. If not all the information is needed on all the documents, then carbon strips are used over only those areas to be reproduced on all forms.

To save further work, carbons of documents are used for internal communications. Here is an example: the invoice shown in Fig. 1.2 is for an order from a furniture manufacturer in High Wycombe to a retailer in London. On receipt of the order, The Successful Manufacturing Co. makes out an invoice and it is typed up in a set of five:

1   the top copy goes to the customer for payment,
2   the second copy goes to the accounts department for book-keeping entries,
3   the third copy goes to the filing department,
4   the fourth copy goes to the warehouse, which releases the goods for despatch,
5   the fifth copy, headed Delivery Note, is sent to the despatch department, which prepares the goods for delivery by the Company's own van. Having served its first purpose, the delivery note is then handed to the delivery man, who in turn hands it to the customer on delivering the goods.

The same procedure can be followed for other sets of documents. In this way all the departments are able to coordinate their efforts to carry out the company's business in the speediest and most efficient manner.

You will have realised by now that the information system is essential for any business. It will often be suggested that it be improved, sometimes that it be streamlined, but never that it be eliminated. The information system is fed by the network of offices throughout the company, and therefore you have a vital task to carry out.

## Office design and layout

If these important purveyors, processors and circulators of information are to work efficiently they must be provided with well-

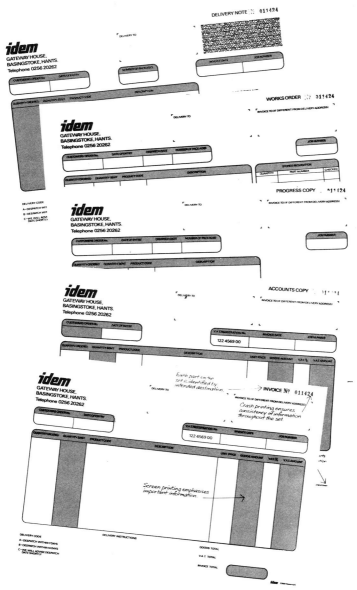

**Fig. 1.3** A typical multi-set of commercial documents (Idem)

designed and carefully planned offices. The same, of course, applies to decision-makers, research staff, designers and others. Everyone, in fact, works better in a clean, warm, well-lit and ventilated environment, furnished in accordance with the tasks to be carried out.

Like so much else, office design has undergone a veritable revolution in the past decade. The changes have been brought about by the need to accommodate new business methods and technology, the need to save space in the face of increasing office rents and the rising cost of energy, and the need for flexibility in a constantly changing business world.

Modern offices are frequently open plan, but with a difference in that screens or screen-hung storage units, sometimes called *carrels*, enclose or partly enclose individual sections or areas, giving the occupants some privacy and protection from noise (see Fig. 1.4). Heating and ventilation are frequently combined in an air-conditioning system. The lighting should not be an array of fluorescent tubes illuminating everything and everybody, but should combine a suitable level of overall lighting, which designers call 'ambient light', with individual lights at desks and other strategic places, which users can switch on and off as they please.

Offices have never before contained so many cables as they do today. In up-to-date offices they are neatly routed in channels along the base and the tops of screens, cabinets, and even desk tops, with outlets at regular intervals. This makes for neatness as well as safety.

The furniture is often system designed – that is, made up of interchangeable parts, rather like Lego bricks – so that you can choose a desk and storage units according to your individual needs from a selection of parts, Each employee will have not only a desk and a chair, but a work station, so that everything you need to get on with your routine work will be near at hand.

As a secretary you might well have an 'L' shaped desk with the section holding your typewriter at a lower level; your main desk will probably incorporate a deep filing drawer, so the files you use every day are always handy; a shallow drawer with slanted horizontal dividers to take your stationery; and a pen tray to hold pens, pencils, paper clips, erasers, typewriter brush, ruler, staples, and so on. (See Fig. 1.5.)

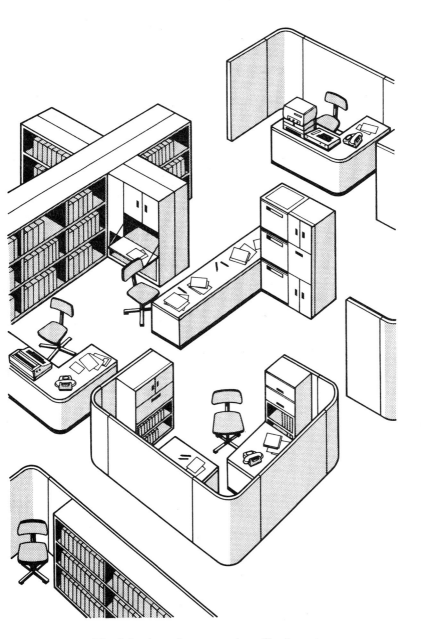

**Fig. 1.4**    A modern open plan office layout

**Fig. 1.5**   A secretary's work station

Your chair is one of the most important items in your work station. If you spend several hours a day at the typewriter, you need a well-designed chair which gives you the support you need in the small of your back. The seat should be adjustable for height so that your feet can rest comfortably on the floor. The back rest should be adjustable both for height and incline towards the body. Arms on chairs are not comfortable for typewriting, unless they are very low.

Finally, you will probably have one or two other storage units to house files, reference books or other material in frequent use.

This modified open plan is a far cry from the original open plan, which came into vogue soon after the Second World War, and extended to houses as well as offices. That kind of open plan really said what it meant, and conceived of the office as one big open space with row upon row of desks with fluorescent lighting overhead. That passed, and this too may pass. Signs are already coming in from Sweden of yet another trend, which takes us one step back – nearer, that is, to the idea of an individual office for everyone. The Swedes call it the *Combi office*. It consists of individual offices for everyone, with a large open area in the centre for meeting, communicating and the service support system.

However, it is imperative to remember that not only are few British offices designed and furnished in the modern idiom, but many of them are still rooted in tradition. Many companies buy their office furniture at second-hand, and many of them did so several years ago, and who knows when they will decide to replace it?

Yet all employers have one obligation and that is to keep within the stipulations of the Offices, Shops and Railway Premises Act 1963. Details of this Act are given in Chapter 16. Suffice it to say here that it stipulates that rooms should be clean, properly lit and ventilated; that after the first hour the temperature should be at least 16°C; that chairs should be suitably designed and constructed; and that each worker must be allotted reasonable space.

**Questions**

1 Define the 'public sector' and the 'private sector'.
2 What is a line executive?
3 Copies of some documents produced in the course of buying and selling are also used as a means of informing internal departments of the progress of transactions with customers and of action to be taken. Mention three such documents, and describe and explain the typical routing of copies.    (LCC PSC Office Organisation and Secretarial Procedures)
4 What points should you consider when selecting a typist's chair?
5 What is a multi-set form, and how is it used?

# 2

# The Role of the Secretary

A secretary's role is to assist and support the chief as well as possible, thereby helping him or her to do a better job. Yet every secretary's job is different, depending on at least four factors: (*a*) whether the office services are centralised or departmentalised; (*b*) to what extent the office services are automated; (*c*) the character and temperament of the employers; and (*d*) the ability and initiative of the individual secretary. The type of business or organisation you are working for can also make a considerable difference to your job.

If you have a job as secretary to the managing director of a small company, you would probably be expected to take care of the running of the entire office. This includes dealing with the incoming and outgoing mail; attending to the correspondence, either taking it down in shorthand or transcribing it from tapes; doing the filing; receiving visitors; dealing with telephone calls; taking care of some figure work; making travel arrangements for your chief, and assisting with meetings. All of these tasks will be dealt with in detail in the following chapters.

The indispensable technical skills required for the job are short-hand and typewriting, an excellent knowledge of English, familiarity with such office routines such as filing, indexing and dealing and with incoming and outgoing mail, and at least some aptitude for figure work. If you can add to this the ability to use such office equipment as a dictating machine or a word processor, or if you are fluent in a foreign language, then your chances of obtaining a good job will be enhanced.

Obviously, you cannot expect to walk straight into a job as

secretary to the managing director. Other qualities are required for the top jobs, but no two experts seem to agree on the exact personal qualities. We analysed three books on secretarial work and found that one author listed no less than twenty-six qualities, the second author was content with nineteen, and the third author settled for nine. The interesting fact is that each of these three experts listed *different* qualities. Only one quality is given by all three – *tact* – so this is obviously important for a secretary. Here are the other qualities listed by any two of the three experts: initiative, conscientiousness, discretion, loyalty and common sense. Only one author mentioned organising ability, yet a secretary could not really manage without it. There is no doubt that other qualities are needed, but rather than putting you off by a long list, we shall deal with them gradually as they arise.

## Acting the part

One of the most important of the personal qualities you will need as a secretary is the ability to get along with others inside the organisation, as well as with callers from the outside. A secretary should be courteous to superiors, colleagues and subordinates alike. When receiving your chief's visitors, you should greet them politely, offer them a seat and generally make sure they are comfortable. If the visitor is early, or your chief delayed, you might offer tea or coffee and something to read. You are not necessarily supposed to entertain visitors with conversation, but if this is called for, you should rise to the occasion.

On no account should you discuss the company's business with visitors, other members of staff, or anyone else. A secretary should know how to be discreet and keep the chief's affairs to herself. You must learn to be secretive without appearing to be, and this requires a knack. Salesmen, competitors, important visitors, other members of the staff – almost anyone, in fact – will often try to 'pump' you, and it is up to you to keep silent without giving offence. Many people use outrageous flattery, and even gifts or luncheon invitations to try to elicit information from secretaries. It would be letting the chief and the company down very badly to succumb.

You will soon discover that every company has its own character and style. Some companies are informal; others rather old-fashioned and formal. It is up to you to adapt, but always bear in mind that it is better to err on the side of formality than otherwise. First names are used a great deal in offices nowadays, and many a secretary calls the chief by his or her first name, particularly when they are both young. Watch your step, though, and do not use a first name unless you are quite sure that it is acceptable. Even if you do usually call your chief by his first name, it is much more businesslike to be formal when visitors are present.

A secretary does not work in a vacuum, attending to the needs of one person, so always bear in mind that you are part of a team or, if you prefer, a series of inter-connecting teams all aiming at the same ultimate goal – the prosperity of the company. This is clearly shown in the organisation chart in Fig. 1.1.

Your chief, and consequently you, will frequently need to liaise or work with some or all of the other departments, and your courtesy and tact can do much to gain the cooperation of others.

## Giving work to others

Almost every secretary sometimes has to give work to others, even if only to the messenger. When doing this, you should proceed in exactly the same way as your chief does, or should do, when he delegates work. Engendering loyalty and enthusiasm in subordinates is not easy, and not all executives do it successfully. Yet the rules are simple and apply equally well all the way down the chain of command:

1   First of all, never be 'bossy'. *Ask* a person to do a job, don't issue orders. If you say to the messenger: 'Would you mind taking this letter down the hall to Mr So-and-So's office, Michael?', he will know perfectly well what he is expected to do, just as you do when the chief rings on the intercom and says: 'Would you mind coming in with your book, June?' It is simply a question of technique.

2   Always give clear instructions. When a job is badly done, it is often because of hasty and confusing instructions. Once you have given instructions on how the job is to be done, ask whether you have been understood and prompt the person being given the work to ask if he has any queries or problems. Many people, particularly youngsters in their first job, are shy to ask questions and need to be

encouraged. It is naturally better to ask than to risk spoiling a batch of work.

3   Giving clear instructions is not to be confused with believing that your own way of doing things is the only valid way and imposing it on everyone else. Certainly house style has to be followed, and most typing jobs have to be done in a certain way, but there are innumerable other office chores which can successfully be dealt with in a number of ways. Let people do them as they wish; *their* way may even be better than yours.

4   Never forget to give appreciation for a job well done. Remember the advice of Dale Carnegie, the famous exponent of *How to Win Friends and Influence People*: 'Be lavish in your praise and unstinting in your appreciation'.

5   On the other hand, it is unenlightened to give anyone a 'dressing down' if they have fallen down on the job. When we make a genuine mistake, we know it all too well and usually feel bad about it. There is no need for a superior to rub it in. Such faults as idleness or unpunctuality, on the other hand, should be dealt with by management.

6   Sometimes it is necessary to ask a person to stay late to finish a job, to delay going to lunch, or otherwise inconvenience himself. Always be as considerate as possible in making such requests and do not do so unless it is absolutely necessary. If overtime is unpaid, allow those working for you to take compensatory time off, if it is within your authority.

7   Do not take advantage of your position to delegate the jobs that you yourself dislike. This will be quite obvious to office juniors and they will naturally resent it.

8   Always be reasonable in your requests. You may know how long it would take you to do a certain job, but bear in mind that a junior will almost certainly take longer. Accuracy should come first, then speed usually follows of its own accord. If you attempt to hurry an inexperienced person, errors and delays will usually result.

9   If a job has gone wrong because your instructions were faulty, apologise sincerely. It will help the person who must do it all again to do so with a good grace.

10  Be loyal to those who work for you. The responsibility for delegated work remains yours. This does not mean that you must accept both blame and praise. It means, rather, that you must pass on the appreciation to whoever did the job, and apologise yourself for any errors made by others – if you have not spotted them in time.

## Office and inter-office relationships

The last thing you will want to do is give the impression of being stand-offish, yet you must try to avoid this while behaving in a suitable way for a responsible office employee. Avoid time-wasting chatter and long sessions in the cloakroom. Do not listen to or spread office gossip, rumours or scandal. If you discourage gossipers, change the subject, get on with your work or move away, people will quickly realise that it is not worth passing on gossip to you and you will very soon be free from the embarrassment of warding them off.

Otherwise, you should strive to be on good terms with everyone with whom you come in contact. It makes work far more pleasant, and it is easier to gain people's cooperation, at any level, if you are on good terms with them.

Ideally, you should be on friendly terms with all, but on intimate terms with no one at the office, because it is very hard to keep the chief's confidential matters from a close friend, or indeed girlfriend or boyfriend. It is also unpleasant for all the details of a romance to become public knowledge at the office, as often happens. None the less, the fact remains that many people do meet their future husbands or wives at their place at work and it is therefore futile to counsel 'ideal behaviour'. The only realistic advice is always to be discreet.

## Getting on with the chief

As for getting on with your chief, the secret is adaptability. Whenever you change jobs, you will have to be prepared to reorient your behaviour entirely to suit the new chief.

All employers are agreed on one point, however: they like their secretary to be neatly dressed and well groomed at all times, for it reflects favourably on them.

Most secretaries quickly learn which is the right moment to approach with a request and when to leave the chief in peace. Some people like sympathetic attention and others prefer to be left alone. By all means be sympathetic on bad days, but don't succumb to the temptation to become too familiar.

People vary considerably in their attitude to privacy. Some ask you to open all their letters, even those marked 'Personal'; others would consider this impertinent. Some people would expect you to retrieve papers from their briefcase as a matter of course, while others would be incensed if you did so. In such matters, therefore, start off by *not* doing the more personal thing. Leave private letters sealed, and if a document is missing and you suspect it might be in his briefcase, say: 'Do you think it might still be in here?' He will then either invite you to have a look, or do so himself. Leave birthdays, wedding anniversaries and other personal matters strictly alone unless asked to provide reminders.

You may find that the chief tells you a great deal about the business and wants to discuss current problems, plans and ideas. If so, pay attention carefully. If your opinion is asked, give it; if not, keep it to yourself. Be enthusiastic about new ideas. Above all, listen intelligently, for you will now be performing one of your most important functions. The 'top' is a lonely place and no one likes to be there without someone in whom to confide plans and hopes for the future, and who can act as a sounding board for ideas and arguments. If your chief has chosen you for this role, then it is a sure sign that your intelligence, wisdom and judgment are appreciated. It is a role which will make you invaluable to your chief, and will also help you to gain much useful knowledge.

**Questions**

1   What is meant by centralised office services, and what are their advantages?
2   Which three qualities are the most important for a secretary?
3   List three of the rules you should follow when giving work to others.
4   You are secretary to Mr Brown, the Sales Manager. At 11.15 a.m. you receive a telephone message from the Managing

Director, summoning Mr Brown to a vital emergency Board Meeting in 15 minutes' time. The meeting will last one hour initially, but will be resumed at 2 p.m. Mr Brown is engaged with an important overseas visitor and has asked not to be disturbed. At noon he had arranged to take the visitor to lunch. His other engagements consist of an interview in his office at 2.15 with one of the sales representatives, and a meeting from 3 p.m. for the rest of the afternoon at another company's premises. What action would you take?　　(LCC PSC Office Organisation and Secretarial Procedures)

# 3

# Organisation and Planning

No one can lay down hard and fast rules on how to organise your day or your work, since how you go about it will depend on how the company is organised, what business it is in, and the kind of chief you have. It will be a question of adapting yourself to the chief's working habits and planning your day accordingly. Certainly some personal organising is essential if you are to fit in the hundred and one things demanded of you. Having organised the day, however, you probably never see it run as smoothly as planned, for there will be constant interruptions – by the telephone, by visitors, or by the chief wanting something done right away. Nothing will go exactly according to plan, yet there must *be* a plan.

## Organising your own work

Most office tasks can be divided into monthly, weekly and daily activities, with others to be done at irregular intervals, such as, for instance, reminders to be sent out ten days before an event, or collection letters to be sent out on the tenth and twenty-eighth day of every month. The types of job to be done monthly will, once again, depend on the business in question and on your own particular job, but they might include billing, making out the monthly payment cheques, preparing the salaries, making up the petty cash, and so on.

   The best way to remind yourself to carry out such tasks at the right time is to note them in your diary in advance. A good time to do it is on completing the current month's task. The same method applies to the one-off task to be performed on a certain day, or those to be performed at irregular intervals. If you send out an invitation or notice of meeting which is to be followed up ten or fifteen days before the event, make a note of the follow-up in the diary when the first mailing goes out. It would be quite unwise to rely on memory for a one-off job in the future.

Tasks to be performed fortnightly or weekly can be handled in the same way, with variations to suit the particular case. If, for instance, stationery is only ordered from stores on Mondays, jot down the words 'Order soft pencils' under Monday's date as soon as you notice stocks getting low. This will save you the unnecessary task of casting around every Monday morning to find out what you need. A file of reminders, called a 'tickler file' is also a useful aid and time-saver. Full details on how to make one up and put it to use are given in Chapter 11.

As for organising your day's work, the most important rule is that your day should fit in with your chief's. There are secretaries who attempt to get their chief to organise the day to suit them and announce that they will come in for dictation as soon as the filing is finished. Such behaviour shows a complete misconception of the role of the secretary.

The suggestions which follow are therefore to be taken simply as basic guidelines. How many of them you adopt will depend on the type of business your company is in and, above all, on the working habits of your chief.

1   Make a good start by arriving five minutes early rather than five minutes late. Go first of all to your chief's desk and make sure all is in order – ash trays empty, pencils sharp, blotter clean, diary open at the right page and desk calendar brought up to date. If there are any dead flowers in the office, remove them. If there is a coffee table with magazines on it, make sure they are straightened out, and yesterday's newspaper either thrown out or filed in its allotted place. Some of these things should have been done by the cleaner, but do not hesitate to use a duster if necessary.

2   In your own office, uncover the typewriter and take out your equipment. Have two sharpened pencils or a pen at the ready, tucked under the rubber band around your shorthand notebook.

Keep the notebook always in the same spot on your desk, and be ready to take dictation at any moment throughout the day.

3    Clean your typewriter, and make sure the type is really clean.

4    Quickly run through your main stationery requirements to make sure nothing is running low. If you jot down requirements in your diary as soon as you notice a shortage, as previously suggested, this check-up will be very minor.

5    Type out a list of visitors expected during the day and send it down to the commissionaire, the receptionist or telephone operator, as applicable. If you make further appointments during the day, do not forget to notify them.

6    When typing the list of callers, notice any other important event for the day and prepare any material needed for it.

7    If you are responsible for opening the chief's mail, do so as soon as it arrives. The mail should always have priority. Open it, date stamp it, read it, and note in your diary and the chief's diary any appointments which are confirmed. If enclosures are mentioned, make sure they are actually in the envelope, and if not, make a pencilled note to that effect on the letter. Follow all the other suggestions made on dealing with the incoming mail (Chapter 4) and place the mail on the chief's desk.

8    Do the filing. Many secretaries find that the chief arrives during the filing, summons her in to take dictation and the filing has to be left. In fact the filing almost always has to be interrupted and you will no doubt learn to accept it as one of the facts of secretarial life. Do, however, make every effort to go back to the filing during the day and to have finished it by the end of the day. If you allow it to accumulate it is very difficult to catch up, and every time the chief wants to refer to a document it takes twice as long to find it.

9    Carry out your other tasks in order of urgency and follow this procedure throughout the day. One of the secretary's greatest assets is the ability to assess priorities. On returning from taking dictation you should do all the urgent mail at once and take it in for signature before lunch. The rest of the mail should be done in the afternoon, so that it can be signed and sent off before the day ends. On the

other hand, some employers prefer to have mail coming in for signature at intervals throughout the day.

## Helping the chief

There is much you can do to help the chief organise the day-to-day work and overall planning. But first of all a word of caution is needed: do not be over-zealous in your efforts to help. Bear in mind that not everyone needs organising, and a constantly prodding secretary can become a thorn in the side of those who can think and remember for themselves. So do be sensitive in this respect.

Anticipate the chief's needs by bringing together all the material needed for an appointment, placing it in a folder, marking it 'Johnson meeting' and putting it on the chief's desk before Mr Johnson arrives. Sort papers into correspondence to be dealt with, material to be read before the next sales meeting, bills to be approved, general reading matter, and so on. Make sure your diary always tallies with his. He will certainly need to turn back to his diary when he comes to make up his expense account and for other reasons too.

## Overall planning

You can also help the chief with the overall planning. Several kinds of control boards and charts can be used for the purposes of reminder, control, statistical record and forward planning. Probably the most common is the Year Planner. There is one on the wall in almost every office. It consists of a large calendar on which forthcoming events such as sales conferences, board meetings and so on can be marked. Different coloured markers, such as stars, discs and squares, are available, so that a different symbol can be used for each event. You might use a red star for board meetings, discs of different colours for several kinds of training sessions, and so on. In this way you would be able to see at a glance what activities have been planned for the year ahead. Year Planners are also used to schedule staff holidays, and in this case charting tape in different colours can be stuck right across the weeks during which a particular member of staff will be on holiday.

The Year Planner is the visual control board at its most simple.

Many more complicated kinds are on the market, some of them so highly mechanised that they can be altered every hour to show changes as they occur. In this way they enable management to keep a constant check on a situation and to make the necessary decisions. Visual control boards are used in production, stock keeping, sales, stores, despatch work, budgeting and for many other purposes.

The main graphs and charts in common use are the following:

**Line graph**

The line graph can be used to illustrate fluctuations and trends in almost any field, such as sales, purchases, profit, dividends, cost of living, population and wages. As shown in Fig. 3.2, line graphs are drawn on graph paper, which is ruled off into 10 mm squares. If needed for a large display, the graph can also be drawn up on a board ruled into squares, or on a peg board. In the first case the lines are 'drawn' with charting tape, and in the second, pegs are inserted into holes in the board. The pegs are joined together with elasticated cord, which forms the lines between the pegs.

**Bar graph**

The bar graph, or histogram, enables you to compare statistics at a glance. The bars can either be drawn individually, each in a different colour or pattern, or else they can be stacked, with each pattern or colour on the same bar representing a different item. Bar charts are usually drawn on chart paper, like line graphs, but can also be created on a large board, using self-adhesive bars or other devices (see Fig. 3.3).

**Pie chart**

A pie chart is a circle, representing the whole, divided into segments. It gives a vivid representation of the relationship of the parts to the whole. The circle or 'pie' could represent each £1 which a manufacturer receives from the sale of his goods. What will the manufacturer do with this pound? Put it in his pocket as profit? Certainly not. The pie chart will inform us that, for instance, 40 per cent of that pound will go to purchase raw materials, another 40 per cent in salaries and wages, 10 per cent in overheads, and a mere 10 per cent is profit. Our local council may also include a pie chart with its rate demands, to show how every pound we pay in rates is spent.

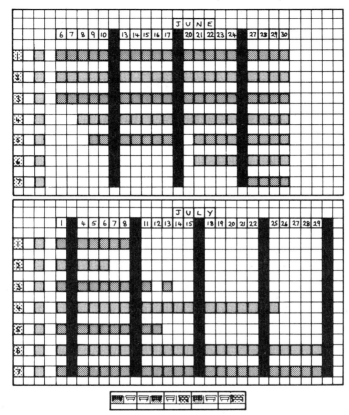

**Fig. 3.1** A visual control board

Pie charts can only give approximate figures and the percentages are not easy to work out, but they do present a very vivid image (see Fig. 3.4).

**Flow chart**

A flow chart illustrates the flow of materials and documents from department to department throughout an organisation until the task in hand is completed. It enables management to study each step in a procedure and decide where improvements are needed. Flow charts are an essential part of system design and are used when devising a computer program for a particular application.

**Pictogram**

A pictogram is a chart using a symbol to indicate a given quantity or number. Half the quantity is represented by half of the symbol, one quarter by a quarter of the symbol and so on. The pictogram is very useful for exhibition work and in advertising, but is not something you would expect to utilise in your office.

## Statistics in action

Let us now imagine that you work for a furniture manufacturer. He asks you to prepare a record of sales broken down into the four lines which the company produces: three-piece suites, kitchen chairs, bedroom furniture and dining-room furniture. He then asks you to provide the total annual profit figures for each product-range for the past five years. You do a neat job of it, using the tabulators on your typewriter or word processor, and the result looks something like this:

*Net profit 19–1 to 19–5 (£)*

|  | 19–1 | 19–2 | 19–3 | 19–4 | 19–5 |
|---|---|---|---|---|---|
| Three-piece suites | 46 030 | 42 000 | 35 100 | 32 600 | 22 260 |
| Kitchen chairs | 16 450 | 16 600 | 13 250 | 14 520 | 15 200 |
| Bedroom furniture | 20 920 | 24 970 | 31 110 | 34 180 | 39 820 |
| Dining-room furniture | 26 270 | 29 800 | 36 730 | 42 500 | 54 170 |
| TOTAL | £109 670 | 113 370 | 116 190 | 123 800 | 131 450 |

Your chief will now have a very clear and accurate picture of the situation. It is clear that the profit from sales of three-piece suites has dropped steadily over the years, while the profit on kitchen chairs has been steady but not spectacular. However, he now wants seriously to consider changing the product 'mix', and wants to consult some colleagues. He therefore asks you to construct a chart which will clearly show the profit trends over the past five years for the four product lines.

Knowing that line graphs are the best medium for illustrating trends and are also quite simple to draw, you should set about preparing one in the following way. Take a piece of graph paper. You will notice that it is ruled off into 10 mm squares. Leaving enough space at the bottom for the title, key and scale, you draw a base line horizontally across the page, then, at regular intervals, you write in each of the five years. Down the left-hand side of the graph you will write in the figures, beginning with £10 000 and moving upwards, £5 000 at a time, until you reach £55 000, which is the highest figure you will need. Each amount belongs alongside one of the thicker lines on your graph paper. Since ten tiny squares separate each thicker line and each of these tiny squares is 1 mm high, the scale will be 10 mm to £5 000. Write this down at the foot of your chart: Scale: 10 mm = £5 000.

Then select four different coloured pencils for the four product lines and write down a key at the foot of the chart – Fig. 3.2 uses contrasting lines instead of colours (which may be more appropriate if your original is to be photocopied). Now you are ready to begin

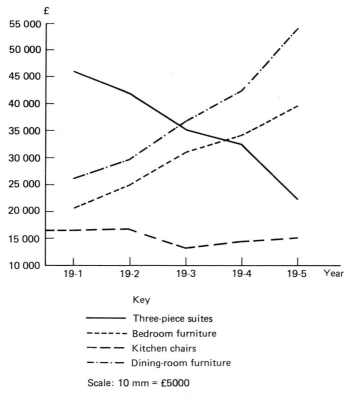

Key

————— Three-piece suites

– – – – – Bedroom furniture

— — — Kitchen chairs

—·—·— Dining-room furniture

Scale: 10 mm = £5000

**Fig. 3.2** A line graph

drawing in the lines. Take the colour selected for three-piece suites. The figure for 19–1 is £46 030. Make a dot at this figure, exactly above 19–1. You will notice that the odd £30 will be lost, since the graph only allows you to get to the nearest £1 000. For 19–2 the figure is £42 000, so make a dot at the appropriate spot over 19–2. Now join up the two dots with a firm pencil line. Proceed in the same fashion for the remaining years and then for the other three product lines. Finally write the title of the chart underneath and label the axes, e.g. £ and Year. Your chart should look rather like Fig. 3.2, but will be more attractive because it will be in colour. Notice how vividly it depicts the falling profitability of three-piece suites, in contrast to the soaring figures for dining-room furniture.

Your chief may well decide to discontinue selling three-piece suites as such, and perhaps consider offering armchairs and settees individually instead. This is, in fact, what many furniture manufacturers have been doing.

You could have made a bar graph, as in Fig. 3.3, to illustrate the figures but this is not as satisfactory as a line graph in this instance, and it would have taken you longer to draw. The original of Fig. 3.3

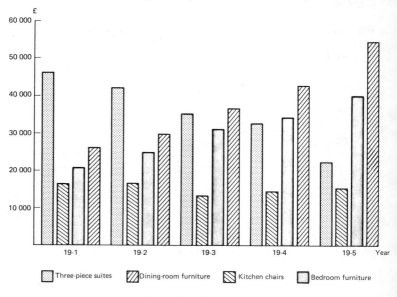

**Fig. 3.3**   A bar chart

was not actually drawn by hand, but by a little machine called a Graphmate. With it you can draw all sorts of graphs simply by touching the right buttons.

Had your chief simply wanted to show the profit figures by product area for one year, you could have drawn up a pie chart like the one in Fig. 3.4. Many companies do this for their annual report. As you will see, this chart shows profits accruing from design consultancy work, as well as from the four different product lines.

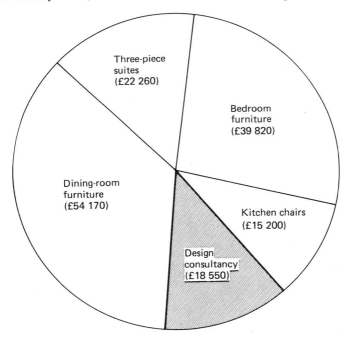

**Fig. 3.4** A pie chart

**Questions**

1   A two-day conference organised by your employer is due to open at 1000 hours tomorrow at the Imperial Hotel in a town 100 miles away. At 1600 hours today you receive a telegram from the opening speaker saying he is ill and unable to attend. Your employer is en route for the Imperial Hotel, which he expects to reach between 1700 and 1730 hours. At 1645 the Imperial Hotel manager telephones to explain that owing to a double booking he has provisionally reserved accommodation for four of the delegates at another hotel in the same group 8 miles from the conference centre. What would you do?     (LCC PSC Office Organisation and Secretarial Procedures)

2   Name one kind of chart most commonly used to display information visually.     (Pitman Secretarial Practice Intermediate)

3   Describe a pie chart and its uses.

4   As a secretary you will have at least two diaries to take care of: your own and your chief's. Describe how these diaries should be used.

5   Opening the chief's mail is a very important task. Describe how it should be done.

# 4

# Handling the Mail

The swift, efficient and discreet handling of both incoming and outgoing mail is one of your most important tasks, even if the volume is small. Like so many other things, the mail, both incoming and outgoing, can be handled either centrally or individually by each department.

Whether you do all the work yourself or handle only your own chief's mail, there are really only differences in volume and degree of mechanisation as far as the actual work is concerned.

## Incoming mail

In a large company the mailroom staff may use a letter-opening machine, sorting frames labelled with the names of the various departments, and shredding machines to dispose of the used envelopes. Once opened and date-stamped, the mail will be sorted according to its final destination, and finally each pile will be put into a folder and delivered to the various departments. Some companies use sorting trolleys into which the mail is dropped into labelled divisions and wheeled straight to the various departments.

Some postrooms deliver all letters unopened to the addressees. We shall assume you work for such a company and that the mail has been placed in your 'In' tray while you are doing the filing. This is your cue to stop what you are doing and attend to the mail right away, taking it in to your chief with the minimum of delay.

If you follow a set routine your task will be easier and you will be sure nothing has been forgotten. Here is the basic procedure:

1   First check through the letters and separate all those marked 'Private', 'Personal' or 'Confidential', and any that may have been misdirected. Advise the postroom right away about misdirected letters. 'Private', 'Personal' and 'Confidential' letters should not be opened unless you have specifically been asked to do so. Some secretaries insist on slitting them open, but it is more considerate not to do so, since most people prefer to open their own personal letters. Just date stamp the envelopes and place them on top of the pile when you have finished sorting the mail.

2   Open all other envelopes and carefully attach any enclosures with a staple.

3   Scan through the letters as you open them, and if they mention an enclosure which you find has been omitted, make a note of the fact at the foot of the letter and sign your statement. For instance, you might write 'Cheque not enclosed'.

4   If the enclosure is a remittance, check to see whether the amount tallies with the one mentioned in the letter. If it is a cheque, make sure it is made out correctly. If there is a discrepancy, make a note to that effect, and sign or initial it. Some companies like all remittances to be recorded in a 'Remittance Book' immediately upon receipt. Some companies also like registered letters to be recorded in a registered mail book. Take care of these details right away.

5   If the letter is from a private individual, make sure his name and address are on it. If not, check to see whether the sender's name and address are on the envelope. If so, attach the envelope to the back of the letter with a staple. Envelopes of letters from abroad should also be attached to the letter since they frequently help in deciphering the address – and the chief may want to keep the stamp!

6   Date stamp all letters, making quite sure you do not obliterate any part of them. It is surprising how many people obliterate a name, an address or even part of the message itself with a date stamp, although there is usually ample space for a date stamp on a letter.

7   Open any postal packets or parcels.

8   Put all newspapers, periodicals and printed matter at the bottom of your pile, followed by the routine correspondence and the most

important letters, with personal and confidential mail on top. If you feel it would help in certain cases, take out the relevant file, clip the incoming letter on top, and put markers on the previous relevant correspondence in the file. In this way the chief can quickly read the previous correspondence to get a complete picture. But do not waste time on this if the chief is already at his desk, as he will almost certainly be impatiently waiting for the mail.

9    So put the incoming mail into a folder with as little delay as possible and place it in the chief's 'In' tray, or follow whatever procedure is customary in your company or preferred by your superior.

Once you have finished your morning stint with the mail, you have not necessarily finished the task for the rest of the day. Express letters, Datapost parcels, overseas telegrams and cables, letters or parcels delivered by private messenger may arrive at any time of the day and have to be dealt with right away, with even greater urgency than the ordinary mail.

## Outgoing mail

The extent to which a secretary has to deal with the outgoing mail depends primarily on the size of the company. In a small company, the secretary may have to take care of the entire mailing operation, with or without help. In other cases she may not even seal the chief's letters. Your own particular situation may well fall somewhere between these two extremes. One thing is certain, however: it is your business to know how the outgoing post should be handled and what kind of services are offered by the Post Office.

If you only have to deal with your own chief's mail, it is a relatively simple operation. You should already have typed a sufficiently large envelope to take all enclosures and separate envelopes or labels for catalogues or samples going out on their own. You should have clipped enclosures behind the letters, so all you will need to do when the mail has returned to your desk after signature is:

1    Make sure that every letter is signed.
2    Check to make sure that names and addresses on letters and

envelopes correspond and are correctly laid out, with the post town in block letters, and including the post code.
3   Put an elastic band around any item to be made into a parcel and the corresponding addressed label, or make a pencilled note on the back of the label of what is to be sent off, e.g. '100 BW Sales leaflets'. Make pencilled notes for any other special piece of mail, such as registered letters or foreign mail.
4   If a messenger collects your mail, all you need to do now is to place it in your 'Out' tray. If there is no mail collection, then take the mail to the postroom yourself.

Your routine will, of course, vary somewhat according to the customary procedure in your company.

If you are working for a small company, the task of handling the outgoing mail for the whole company may well fall upon you, or you may have to take responsibility for the operation while a junior clerk takes care of the details. In such a case you will need a well organised routine to ensure that everything goes off smoothly. Get a copy of the *Post Office Guide* and the latest leaflets on the inland and overseas postal rates. Between them, these publications will provide you with all the information you need about available services, postage rates, the time it takes for mail to reach destinations by the various methods, how to tie a parcel, and so on. You should then proceed as follows:

1   Set a deadline for letters to be handed in to you if they are to catch the day's post.

2   Check to make sure that names and addresses on letters match those on the corresponding envelopes and that all indications, such as 'Special Delivery' or 'For the attention of Mr Jones' also appear on the envelopes.

3   Type out any labels or envelopes for catalogues and so on which may have been left undone. Gradually you should be able to persuade the typists to remember to take care of such extra details when typing the letters.

4   Fold all letters, insert them into their envelopes, together with any enclosures, seal them or tuck in the flaps as required. Deal with all envelopes for catalogues at the same time, but leave small parcels until later.

5   Separate out all special mail, such as registered letters, special delivery letters, foreign mail or other mail requiring labels to be made out, small parcels to be made up, and so on, then divide the bulk of the mail into first and second class.

6   Weigh and stamp each letter, using the franking machine if one is provided, and making use of your *Post Office Guide* or the other leaflets if you are unsure of the rate applicable.

7   Deal next with the special mail. Parcels must be well packed to protect the contents from damage in transit. Use a box or corrugated paper well sealed down with self-adhesive tape. Then wrap the item in stout brown paper, stick on the label, and either tie it with string or seal it with adhesive tape. For registered parcels, every knot where the string crosses has to be sealed with wax. The contents of all parcels sent abroad must be declared and the appropriate forms are available from the Post Office. Very full details on how to deal with all these special items of mail are given in the *Post Office Guide*.

8   Tie letters in bundles of first and second class mail with the addresses all facing the same way, but still keep all special mail separate. If your local post office asks you to tie up letters in any particular way, then follow their recommendations.

9   Hand the mail over to the person taking it to the post office, with careful verbal instructions about the special mail. If you have used a franking machine you will have to deliver the mail to a specific post office or post it in a special envelope in a post-box agreed with the Head Postmaster. If your company does use a franking machine, get a copy of the Post Office poster 'How to Post Franked Mail'. In addition you will have to keep a control card showing the reading on the meter at the end of each working day, and present it to the Post Office once a week. You will also have to take care of changing the date on the machine every day, cleaning the type and making sure there is an adequate supply of ink in the machine.

10   If you are using a franking machine you will have an automatic record of the postage used, but if letters are stamped by hand you will need to keep a post book. Some companies insist on keeping a record of every letter which goes out, while others – the great

majority – settle for an account of the total postage used each day, with only special letters and parcels accounted for individually.

If your company sends out over one thousand pieces of mail a day, the Post Office will collect it from you daily without charge. The same applies to parcels in lots of twenty or more at a time. If your mail is quite small normally, but you have a large mailing two or three times a year, you can arrange for it to be collected on these occasions only. A telephone call to the Post Office is all that is necessary, but then there is a small charge.

## Mailing in the electronic age

In theory, at least, most of what we have said about outgoing mail is already out-of-date, for the electronic age has transformed the postroom. There are now electronic scales which give you an instant digital read-out of the weight and exact postage rate required. All you need to do is to put your envelope on the scale and select 'First Class', 'Second Class', 'Swiftair', 'Registered', etc., by touching the appropriate key.

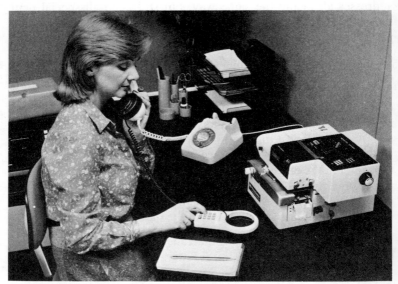

**Fig. 4.1**   A remote meter resetting system (Pitney Bowes)

The first electronic postage meter has appeared on the market and franking machines can now be reset by remote control. Fig. 4.1 shows the Pitney Bowes Remote Meter Resetting System, which permits postage meters to be reset by telephone. There are even computerised mailing systems which separate continuous forms, fold, insert, seal and frank.

**Dialcom**

A major development is British Telecom's Electronic Mail service. It is based on an inter-terminal communication system developed and operated in the USA. It is known as Dialcom and is run on Prime 750 computers. Users link up to it by dialling it over the telephone or by using Telecom's Packet Switched Data Service.

Once connected, the sender uses his own terminal – keyboard printer, visual display unit, word processor or Prestel equipped with full alphanumerical keyboard – as an ordinary typewriter. Letters or memoranda are typed out, as well as the 'address' for correspondence intended for another user of the service, for instance a fellow employee in another office. The computer then 'delivers' the correspondence to the destination terminal, alerting the recipient that mail is waiting as soon as the terminal is switched on.

Urgent correspondence can be given a priority coding and would then be presented to the recipient ahead of other material waiting to be read. A sender can also add a 'Reply Requested' code which requests the recipient to respond before dealing with other mail awaiting attention.

Correspondence can also be sent simultaneously to several destinations, thus eliminating the chore of taking multiple copies and addressing them individually for delivery through the internal mail.

British Telecom recommend the Dialcom service for large and medium-sized companies with offices in several locations, as well as for customers abroad on different Dialcom systems. It is already in use in Britain and the number of users will no doubt increase.

Meanwhile, here are some of the more down-to-earth aids for the postroom of a large company:

*Addressing machines and systems*    Addressing machines print out addresses on envelopes, labels, invoices, statements, postcards, leaflets and payslips. Basically they consist of a master – that is, the address itself, typed or otherwise reproduced – a storage or filing method for the addresses, and the equipment which does the actual printing. Addressing machines have been in use for a good many years and consequently the range extends from the simple manual machine to the micro-based computerised system. Further details are given in Chapter 14.

*Collators*   These are machines for assembling the pages of long documents. They can be manual or electrically operated and are available in various sizes.

*Joggers*   These machines jog papers placed on them into neat piles ready for stapling.

*Perforators*   As the name indicates, these contraptions punch holes in the margins of sets of papers ready for binding.

*Folding machines*   These are available in a number of sizes and can be adjusted to give different types of fold. Some tuck one folded sheet inside another for mailing without envelopes.

*Inserters*   These collate, fold, insert into the envelope, then seal and stack the envelopes. There are several versions of these machines, each offering added facilities until the ultimate is reached in the computerised system.

*Tying machines*   These tie string around parcels and bundles of envelopes.

*Sealers*   Whereas you may use a damp sponge at the end of a tube or a roller passing through water to moisten your envelopes, the large postroom may well use a machine which moistens, seals and stacks the envelopes all in one smooth, electrically-driven operation.

*Multi-purpose franking machines*   We have already touched on the effect of the electronic age on the franking machine, but there is more to come. There are now franking machines which produce self-adhesive labels and which automatically feed, seal and frank the envelopes, neatly stacking them on completion.

On a much more mundane level, sorting frames can be used to separate mail prior to franking. Pigeon-holes can be reserved for first class, second class, London, country, abroad, and packets. Finally, it is useful to have a hook fitted to hold the mail bags upright, or one of the wheeled trolleys which take two bags.

# Postal services

The Post Office offers an almost bewildering choice of services and it pays to take care to select the one most appropriate to the piece of mail you are sending. Sometimes speed is essential, at other times a low postage rate may be more important, or you may require proof of posting, proof of delivery or indeed both. All of these services and many more are available. The *Post Office Guide*, which can be ordered from main post offices and from HM Stationery Office, lists all the available services, as well as other useful information. The up-to-date postal rates are given in two booklets, one for inland mail and the other for overseas mail, available free of charge from any post office. Very briefly, the main services available are the following:

**First-class letter post**   For urgent mail, first-class letter post should be used. The Post Office states that mail sent by this service will 'normally' be delivered on the first working day after collection. No weight limit is specified, but the size must not exceed 610 mm (24 inches) in length, 460 mm (18 inches) in width, and 460 mm (18 inches) in depth. The Post Office also recommends the use of 'Post Office Preferred' (POP) envelopes and cards. They should be oblong in shape with the longer side at least 1·414 times the shorter side and should be made from paper weighing at least 63 grams per square metre (see Chapter 6). It is not necessary to write 'First Class' or 'Second Class' on an envelope which has already been stamped to the correct value.

**Second-class letter post**   This costs a little less, but takes a little longer – sometimes much longer, it has to be admitted. Second-class letters should not weigh more than 750 g. All inland letters should be sealed.

**Unstamped letters**   If a letter is posted unpaid or underpaid, it is treated as a second-class letter and is charged on delivery with double the amount of the deficit of second-class postage. This is known as 'Surcharge'. A letter posted with less than first-class postage is treated as a second-class letter.

**Bulk mail**   Second-class letters posted in bulk can qualify for rebates of postage. The minimum number of letters required in order to qualify for a rebate is 4 251. A number of other conditions has to be fulfilled, yet this method of posting is worth investigating for companies which have large mailings of advertising material or other matter. See the *Post Office Guide* for full details.

**Articles for the blind**   Packets containing letters, books or other literature for the blind, and not weighing more than 7 kg, are delivered free of charge.

**Recorded delivery**   This service provides a record of posting and delivery, with limited compensation cover in the event of loss or damage in the post. This service can be used for all sorts of postal packets, except parcels, railway letters and parcels, airway letters and cash on delivery packets. A fee in addition to the ordinary postage must be paid. All you do is to write the name and address on a form supplied by the Post Office, detach one end and stick it to the packet, above and towards the left, and hand in both the packet and form at the post office counter, together with the appropriate postage. The clerk stamps the form and returns it to you. You can conveniently attach this certificate of posting to the carbon of the corresponding letter. Recorded delivery packets travel in the ordinary unregistered post and are given no special treatment, except that a receipt is taken on delivery and kept at the delivery office.

**Registration**   The registration service can be used for all first-class letters, except airway and railway letters or parcels. It provides for compensation in case of loss. The registration fee varies according to the compensation required and you should consult the *Post Office Guide* for full details. Registered letters have to be handed in to the post office counter and a receipt obtained. Special reinforced envelopes in various sizes can be obtained from post offices for registered letters. Packages must comply with certain regulations and there are also limitations regarding content which should be checked.

**Railway letters**   You can hand a letter weighing not more than 60 g to a railway official at your local station, to be called for on arrival. Or you can address the letter to the addressee's full postal address and the railway staff will post it in the nearest post-box on arrival. The letter should be stamped for first-class postage and in addition there is a railway fee, payable in cash to the official to whom the letter is handed. If you wish to use this service, enquire beforehand at your nearest station.

**Airway letters** Much the same arrangement applies to letters going via British Airways. The letter must not weigh more than 500 g and has to be stamped for first-class mail. It is then handed over to the airport office, where an additional fee is paid. The letter is conveyed on the next available direct flight, to be called for at the airport or transferred to the ordinary post by the airline. Before using this service, get in touch with your nearest British Airways office.

### Royal Mail special services
Consider one of the following for your urgent mail:

**Datapost** This is a fast and reliable overnight delivery service for urgent packages. It is available nationwide and to most overseas countries, either on a contractual basis or over the counter.

**Special delivery** This service provides delivery by Post Office messenger for letters and packets arriving at a delivery office on the next working day after posting, but too late for normal delivery on that day. An additional fee has to be paid, which is refunded if delivery is not achieved on the next working day.

**Swiftair** This is a high-speed overseas letter post. Special handling ensures that it leaves on the first available flight, with fast delivery at its destination, in some cases by special messenger.

**Expresspost** This is a fast messenger collection and delivery service available in London and certain other large towns.

**Intelpost** This is not really a postal service in the conventional sense, but a facsimile transmission service like those described at the end of the next chapter. Document facsimiles are transmitted by satellite to Toronto, Washington and New York and via landline link with eighteen centres in the United Kingdom and Amsterdam. Participating post offices display the 'Intelpost' sign.

For companies wishing to encourage replies to their advertisements or direct mail advertising campaign, the Post Office offers the following three services:

**Business reply service**   The advertiser encloses an unstamped reply card, letter card, label or envelope in the Post Office's official design. The addressee can use the enclosure to reply without adding a stamp and the postage is paid by the advertiser, who also has to obtain a licence from the Post Office.

**Freepost**   This service saves the cost of printing reply cards, and is useful in cases where it is not possible to enclose a card, such as, for instance, in television or radio advertising. The user first obtains a licence from the Post Office and agrees a special abbreviated address with the Head Postmaster to which all the Freepost letters should be sent. The word Freepost is always included in the address.

**Admail**   This service enables advertisers to give a local address in their advertisements and to have replies redirected to their head office or warehouse. It can be combined with the Freepost service.

### Overseas post

There is only one class of mail available for letters within Europe. The Post Office calls it 'All-up', and states that despatch is by air whenever this will result in earlier postal delivery. For countries outside Europe, there is an airmail service and a surface mail service, as well as special rates for printed papers and small packets. Letters may also be sent on the special Aerogramme form available from the Post Office. The Post Office booklet *Overseas Compendium* gives full details of the overseas service, including postal rates for all countries, Customs and VAT requirements for packages, and everything else you need to know.

Airmail letters should bear the blue 'Air Mail' label, available from the Post Office. If you run out of them, you can write the words clearly on the top left-hand corner of the envelope.

**Reply coupons**   If you want to pre-pay for a reply to a letter sent abroad, you enclose a reply coupon, purchased from the Post Office. The addressee then exchanges the coupon at his Post Office for the correct postage. Correspondents abroad can do the same.

### Parcels

Small parcels can be sent at the first-class or second-class letter rates or as Compensation Fee parcels (CF). This involves the payment of an additional fee, which ensures compensation, according to the fee paid, in case of loss or damage in the post. Parcels can also be sent by Datapost or Expresspost. The Post Office has a very comprehensive parcel post service and you should obtain a copy of the booklet *Royal Mail Parcels* for further details.

We have now entered a period of intense competition in all fields and no doubt competition will intensify in the future. You should therefore be aware that it is possible to send a parcel otherwise than through the Post Office. British Rail runs a parcel service and you can obtain a leaflet giving details at your nearest railway station. There is also a number of private package-delivery services, such as Courier-Express and Securicor Parcels Service. To send goods abroad on a regular basis, one normally uses the services of a freight forwarding agent. Addresses are to be found in the yellow pages of the telephone directory.

**Questions**
1  Choose five of the following items and state which Post Office service you would choose for the despatch of each one. Give your reasons:
 (*a*) Sending a letter to a customer making a final request for payment.
 (*b*) Mailing sales literature to potential customers so that they are encouraged to reply.
 (*c*) Despatching 10 000 circulars to customers and suppliers, notifying them of a change of premises.
 (*d*) Forwarding the office cleaner's weekly wages to her home as she is away sick.
 (*e*) Sending computer data daily from a branch to Head Office.
 (*f*) Providing £50 which is required by a branch office today.
 (*g*) Sending goods to a small customer who has no credit facilities with your company.
 (*h*) Despatching a prototype quartz-crystal radio/clock to a designer (value £100).   (LCC PSC Office Organisation and Secretarial Procedures)
2  Name two items other than postal rates you would need to know if you are sending a parcel abroad.   (Pitman Secretarial Practice Intermediate)

3   Describe how electronic scales, franking machines and Dialcom are used in the modern mailroom.
4   What is the difference between Recorded Delivery and Registered Post?
5   Give two ways of sending parcels other than through the Post Office. What are the advantages of these methods?
6   What literature is available from the Post Office to help you in handling the mail?
7   You are secretary to the sales manager. It is the end of the working day and you have just collected the signed mail from his 'Out' tray. How will you deal with it before the messenger calls to take it to the mailroom?

# 5

# Written and Visual Communications

A large amount of time in business is spent communicating with other people. Asking a messenger to deliver a parcel, selling a multi-million pound plant to an overseas customer, writing a memo to the staff about the new office hours and drawing up a contract for a new development are all exercises in communication. Telephoning the corner shop for a sandwich, showing a training film to the sales force, running a Board meeting and writing a telegram are also all exercises in communication. Although they are not all equally important, each must be done correctly if the desired results are to be obtained.

It follows that everyone in business must have some skill in communications. The better you are at communicating, the more likely you are to make a success of your job. This applies particularly to the secretary, who has a very complex communications job to do.

## Written English

The ability to express yourself in clear concise English, free from grammatical errors and from jargon, is one of the greatest assets for a secretary. It is your business to see that every letter or document you place before your chief is free from spelling mistakes. If you are not sure of a spelling, look it up in the dictionary. No secretary's desk should be without a dictionary, and if one is not provided, you should ask for one without hesitation.

Be especially wary of those words you *think* you know how to spell. Two or more words often sound alike, but are spelled differently and have different meanings. Here is a short list of some of the most common:

| Word | Meaning or definition |
| --- | --- |
| Abjure | Renounce on oath |
| Adjure | Charge or request solemnly |
| Adapt | Suit, fit |
| Adopt | Take over |
| Advice | (noun) Opinion, counsel |
| Advise | (verb) To offer an opinion |
| Affect | Influence |
| Effect | Accomplish, result |
| Allusion | Reference |
| Illusion | Deception |
| Alternate | Occurring by turns |
| Alternative | Choice between two or more things |
| Ante | Before |
| Anti | Against |
| Apprise | Inform |
| Apprize | Set value on |
| Calendar | Table of dates |
| Colander | Strainer |
| Canvas | Cloth |
| Canvass | Solicit, sell |
| Carat | Unit of weight |
| Caret | Printer's mark |
| Carrot | Vegetable |
| Censer | Incense-burning vessel |
| Censor | (noun) Official; (verb) to suppress |
| Complacent | Self-satisfied |
| Complaisant | Disposed to please |
| Complement | Supplement |
| Compliment | (verb and noun) Praise |
| Council | Meeting, body |
| Counsel | (noun) Advice, adviser; (verb) to advise |
| Dependant (of) | (noun) One who depends |
| Dependent (on) | (adj) Relying on, depending on |
| Depositary | Person to whom something is entrusted |

| | |
|---|---|
| Depository | Place where something is deposited |
| Deprecate | Express disapproval of |
| Depreciate | Diminish in value |
| Descendant (of) | (noun) Person descended from |
| Descendent | (adj) Descending, going down |
| Draft | (noun) Rough copy of document |
| Draught | (noun) Breeze; (verb) draw |
| Envelop | (verb) To enclose, embrace |
| Envelope | (noun) Stationery |
| Equable | Even |
| Equitable | Fair, just |
| Farther | More distant |
| Further | Additional |
| Forego | Precede (also give up) |
| Forgo | Give up |
| Gaol | Prison, jail |
| Goal | End, aim |
| Jam | (noun) Conserve; (verb) pack |
| Jamb | Doorpost |
| Licence | (noun) Permission |
| License | (verb) To permit |
| Loath | (adj) Reluctant |
| Loathe | (verb) To hate |
| Practice | (noun) Action, method |
| Practise | (verb) To act, carry out |
| Presumptive | Probable |
| Presumptuous | Insolently assuming |
| Principal | (adj) Chief, main; (noun) head |
| Principle | Rule, tenet |
| Stationary | (adj) Still, motionless |
| Stationery | (noun) Letterheads, envelopes, etc. |

Having taken a firm stand with regard to spelling, in the matter of *style* you must be prepared to be flexible and adapt to your chief. Some people expect you to transcribe letters exactly as dictated; others expect you to tidy up their grammar and other lapses; a third group will expect you to make any alterations which lead to a smoother, clearer letter.

It is your job as a secretary to adapt to your chief's particular wishes. If you make corrections, do it unobtrusively, and tamper as little as possible with the original. Resist the temptation to impose your own style on the letters.

The right kind of chief will gradually let you take care of some of the routine correspondence yourself and to write almost any letter from the briefest outline. When you come to writing your own letters, bear in mind the following hints.

## Brevity and simplicity

Brevity and simplicity are the key to good written English, and are frequently the same thing, as short words are often the simplest words. Many people believe that a longer word is more impressive and that they will lose face if they stick to the short homely ones, but nothing could be further from the truth. No less an authority than Sir Ernest Gowers said 'Those who run to long words are mainly the unskilled and tasteless. They confuse pomposity with dignity, flaccidity with ease, and bulk with force.'

Try to avoid peppering your letters with long words having prefixes and suffixes of foreign origin, such as *pre*, *re*, *de* or *ousness* and *isation*. You will frequently find a shorter word will serve your purpose equally well, if not better. You may also discover that simplicity and clarity are not so easy to achieve as you may have thought!

This does not mean, of course, that all short words are necessarily better just *because* they are short. You also need the *right* word. Some short words are over-used and have become almost meaningless – for example the word *nice*, which can describe a 'nice girl', a 'nice steak', a 'nice garden' and even a 'nice salary'. You would do better to decide exactly what you mean and find a word which conveys it precisely.

The best way to do this is to use a dictionary. If you think you have the word you want, look it up: you may be surprised to discover what it really means. Another useful aid is *Roget's Thesaurus*, which contains lists of words with similar meanings. If a word does not seem exactly right, you can look it up and choose an alternative from the list provided. You should eventually find a word which conveys exactly what you want to say, and your knowledge of words and their meanings will gradually increase, so that your writing becomes more precise.

As well as short words you should favour short sentences. This will give your writing a more up-to-date style and make it easier to read and understand. Several studies have been made over the years to establish what makes a piece of writing easy to read and they have often concluded that it is the short sentence.

Apart from using short words, the way to write short sentences is to use *fewer* words – that is, fewer words to say the same thing. Have you ever realised how many surplus words most of us allow into our sentences? If you try a pruning operation on your next piece of prose, you will discover this for yourself. Read over every sentence and ask yourself: 'Is this word really necessary? Will the meaning change if I throw it out?' If the answer is 'No', then always remove the surplus word. Your writing will gain in clarity and conciseness by this process.

Superfluous words are hard to eliminate, however, and they will only go by a determined effort on your part. At first you will feel that there is not a single word too many in your letters and will defend every one. However, by looking carefully at the page, going back to the beginning and reading through again, surely enough you will find the redundant words will begin to stand out, and beg to be deleted. Be ruthless about it, for there is no room for surplus words in a crisp piece of writing.

## The cliché

You should avoid the specimens of 'Commercial English' which still haunt far too many business letters. Eliminate them from your own letters, however, not from other people's, unless heavy editing is expected of you.

Here is a list of expendable clichés:

and oblige (as a close)
as and from
as per
as stated above
assuring you of our best attention
at an early date
at hand

at the present time
at this writing
avail yourself of this opportunity
await the pleasure of a reply
awaiting the favour of your
   further esteemed commands

beg to acknowledge
beg to advise
beg to remain (before com-
    plimentary close)

carefully noted
communication (instead of let-
    ter)
complying with your request
contents duly noted

deem it advisable
desire to state
due to the fact that

esteemed favour
even date

favour (meaning a letter)

has come to hand
has gone forward
have before me
having regard to the fact
herewith please find
hoping to be favoured

if and when
in answer to same
in connection therewith
in reply to yours
in reply I wish to state
in the not too distant future
in this connection
instant (meaning this month)

kind favour
kindly advise
kindly be advised
kindly inform

note with interest
note with pleasure

of even date
owing to the fact that

past favours
permit me to state
please be advised
please rest assured
proximo (for next month)
pursuant to

referring to your favour
referring to yours
replying to your favour
replying to yours

said (e.g. said package)
same (used as a pronoun)
submit herewith

take pleasure in advising
thank you kindly
the writer (instead of I)
trusting this will

ultimo

valued favour
valued patronage

we take pleasure
well and truly
when and as
wherein we state

your esteemed communication
your esteemed favour
your favour to hand
your goodself
your letter of even date
your valued inquiry
yours just to hand
yours of the fourth
yours to hand

## Word division

The most important rule about word division is to avoid it if you possibly can. The following are never divided:

1 *One-syllable words* such as: bought, straight, gone.
2 *Hyphenated words* should be divided only at the point of hyphenation, e.g. sub- committee, vice- president.
3 *Proper names*  Names of persons and places are not divided, unless they are compound names. Neither should initials or qualifications be separated from a surname.
4 *Foreign words* used in English writing are not divided, e.g. *directeur, fabbrica, universidad*.
5 *Dates*  The day and the month, as well as the year, if possible, should appear on the same line.

If you *must* divide a word, then the rules to follow are these:

1 *Compound words*  Divide between the two elements, e.g. rail-way, air-line, sub-marine. If a word has more than two elements, it is best to divide it at the second point, e.g. discre-tion, perpen-dicular.
2 *Syllables*  As a general rule, words should be divided according to the syllables which make them up, e.g. busi-ness, candi-date. Each syllable following a break usually begins with a consonant, with two exceptions: 'r' accompanies a preceding vowel, and vowel suffixes must be kept together. Thus we have intoler-ant, gener-ally, and hop-ing and depend-ant.
3 *Prefixes and suffixes*  Words containing a prefix or a suffix divide at that point, e.g. pre-determine, explo-sion.
4 *Double vowels*  Words with two adjacent vowels can be divided between the two vowels if the first part of the word sufficiently suggests the second part, e.g. sixti-eth, industri-ous.
5 *Double and treble consonants*  Words with double consonants are usually divided between the two consonants. Words with three consecutive consonants are usually divided after the first. This also includes words with a suffix where the final consonant is doubled. Thus we have duel-ling, circum-stance and dis-miss, respectively.

The best rule of all is: if in doubt, don't divide!

## Capital letters

The current trend is to cut down on the use of capital letters, but they should be used in the following:

1   Proper names of persons, countries, towns, cities, villages, counties, rivers, mountains, lakes, seas and oceans.
2   The names of the month and days of the week.
3   The titles of books, plays, articles, magazines, chapters in books, speeches, operas, songs, etc. Examples are: 'He wrote a play called *Ghosts*'; 'The book is called *Teach Yourself Spelling*.'
4   The names of ships, houses, hotels, restaurants, inns, theatres, etc.
5   A common noun when it is used in conjunction with a proper noun, e.g. Regent Street, Mount Whitney, Waterloo Bridge. Likewise when a common noun is used in place of a proper name, e.g. 'The Company declared a dividend of 87p', since, obviously, a specific company is meant.
6   A designation of rank or position when it is used in conjunction with a proper name, e.g. 'Colonel Harris has resigned his commission'. The same rule applies when the designation refers to a particular person, e.g. 'The Duke has returned from his summer residence.'

Do *not* use capital letters for the following:

1   A common noun when it is used to indicate a general category of person or thing, e.g. 'There are many colleges and universities in the country'.
2   A designation of rank or position when it is used as a common noun, e.g. 'Many of our branch managers have worked their way up from the bottom'.
3   The names of the various disciplines when used in a general sense, e.g. 'He read history and economics'.

You may well find that your employer has certain preferences in the matter of when to use capital letters, or the company you work for may have a house style of its own. Furthermore, some professions, such as the legal profession, have their own customs, not merely with regard to capital letters but in many other stylistic matters as well. In such cases you will obviously act accordingly.

If the matter is left entirely to you, then the above suggestions should help. Once you have adopted a certain style, then use it consistently in all your work.

## Punctuation

The trend is towards less use of punctuation marks, yet the subject is important, since a misplaced comma can change the entire meaning of a sentence. The removal of all commas can make a sentence difficult to understand, as you may have noticed in your reading.

Punctuation marks indicate pauses of different lengths, and so they help to define, clarify or emphasise what has been written.

Here is a guide to the correct use of punctuation marks:

### Full stop

The full stop is used at the end of a sentence, and since the trend is towards shorter sentences, the full stop is in frequent use. It is not used if the sentence is in the form of a direct question, when it ends in a question mark, nor if it is an exclamation, when it ends with an exclamation mark, but you will very rarely have occasion to use exclamation marks in a business letter. The full stop is also used after initials and many abbreviations. Nowadays, however, there is a tendency to leave out stops after initials in the interests of speed. If an abbreviation ends as the word normally would, then no full stop is necessary. Hence we have Dec., Tue., B.C., but Dr, Mr, Mme. Technically, the latter are contractions rather than abbreviations.

### Comma

This indicates the shortest pause of all and was once used extensively, but is not so common now, partly because of the advent of the shorter sentence. Do not make the mistake of dispensing with it completely, however, for its presence is often vital. If the omission of a comma alters your meaning, or if it makes the sentence harder to understand, then you should put one in.

More specifically, use a comma in the following cases:

1   To separate a short list of items, e.g. 'Our salesman will show you samples of carbon paper, typewriter ribbons, shorthand notebooks, and other accessories'. If you are listing only two

items, then no comma is needed, e.g. 'Kith and kin'. The same treatment is given to lists of other kinds, such as adjectives.

2   To mark off a vocative or salutation from the main part of a sentence, e.g. 'I tell you, Sir, this is true'.

3   To separate parenthetic clauses from the rest of the sentence, and to separate words or phrases in apposition, e.g. 'Mr Jones, whom I believe you have already met, will be joining us shortly'.

A comma need *not* necessarily be used to separate off such words as 'However' or short phrases such as 'at this point'. It is perfectly correct to write: 'I will not however speak of his conduct on that occasion' or 'I introduce you at this point to a new character'. Many writers do like to place 'however' and 'therefore' between commas, though, and you should follow your chief's wishes.

### Semicolon

This punctuation mark indicates a pause somewhat shorter than a full stop, yet longer than a comma. The modern trend to shorter sentences has reduced its use, especially in business letters. If you write sentences so long as to need subdivision with semicolons, you would probably do better to recast them into several short sentences.

There are occasions, however, when the use of the semicolon makes for easier reading or greater clarity. Do not hesitate to make use of it on such occasions. If you are listing several items, for instance, and want to describe each one of them briefly, use the semicolon to divide the broad categories, and commas to separate the items within each category. But first announce your list, followed by a colon, e.g.: 'We have quite a large typing pool: Miss Smith, Miss Jones, and Miss Watson who take care of the Sales Department; Miss Brown, Miss Duckworth, and Miss Wells who work for the Production Department; Mrs Rogers and Miss Greene who work mainly for the Accounts Department; and Mrs Wilson who helps all round'. Although this is a very long sentence, it is perfectly clear, thanks to the correct punctuation.

Sometimes the semicolon definitely indicates a longer pause. This often happens when you leave out a word. For instance, if you write: 'We have six men to cover England and Wales, but only one to cover the whole of Scotland', a comma will do admirably. If you omit the 'but', a longer pause will be called for and a semicolon will serve the purpose better: 'We have six men to cover England and Wales; only one to cover the whole of Scotland.'

## Colon

The colon indicates a pause somewhat longer than a semicolon, but not quite so long as a full stop. You will seldom need to use it in business letters, but it can be useful before a direct quotation instead of a comma. The more common use for the colon, however, is to introduce a list, examples or explanations (see page 60), e.g. 'All new employees are given the following: a locker, an overall, a pair of safety shoes, and a "Welcome" booklet' – or in emphasising a contrast, e.g. 'Jones got six orders: Smith only got one'.

## Question mark

The question mark is used after a direct question, but never after an indirect one, e.g. 'Has John arrived yet?' but 'He asked me whether John had arrived'. A question mark can also be used between parentheses to indicate that a word or statement is in doubt. This is sometimes acceptable in reports or memoranda, but never in a letter.

## Exclamation mark

Use this very sparingly in a business letter, if at all. It should be used only in a genuine exclamation, such as: 'Hallo, there!' a 'Watch your step!' It indicates command, surprise or strong emotion.

## Inverted commas

These are used before and after direct speech. If you have a quotation within a quotation, then use double inverted commas for the first one, and single inverted commas for the second. The reverse order can be used if you wish, provided that you are consistent.

Inverted commas, either single or double, are also used to enclose the titles of books, plays, operas, songs; the names of inns, restaurants, hotels, etc. In print, however, such names are usually in italics and not within inverted commas.

**Parentheses**

Parentheses, or brackets as they are usually called, are used to enclose a brief explanation, a reference or an aside with a secondary bearing on the subject. They are not much used in business correspondence, except for enumerating items, e.g. (1), (2), (3) and so on. Do bear in mind, however, that brackets are not a substitute for other punctuation marks and if you *do* use them, they should be inserted without changing the existing punctuation.

Brackets are used a great deal in scientific and similar papers and also in legal documents. Where both figures and words have to be typed, brackets are often used, e.g. £200 (two hundred pounds).

**Hyphen**

Your typewriter has only one key for the hyphen and the dash. They are none the less two quite different punctuation marks. The hyphen is used mainly for two purposes: to separate a word when you have reached the end of a line, and to unite two separate words into a compound one. The rules for separating words have already been given on p. 57. Compound words have a complication of their own and it stems from the fact that English is a live language which is developing all the time. Today's separate word meets and is linked with another one and becomes a compound word, and so the two words are united with a hyphen. Often they then become one word and no longer need a hyphen, e.g. multinational. Some people remove nearly all hyphens in anticipation; others prefer to observe conventions.

So what should you do? Neither approach can be dismissed as incorrect. The only answer is to be consistent, and the way to do this is to be guided by an up-to-date dictionary.

**Dash**

This should in reality be longer than the hyphen, but on a typewriter you have no choice but to use the same key as for the hyphen. Strictly speaking, a dash should be used only to signify a sudden break in the reasoning, the resumption of an interrupted subject or an omission. Here are some examples:

'. . . and his name was – well, I can't tell you what it was.'

Adaptability, loyalty, industry – these are the qualities needed in a secretary.

The report stated mysteriously that the *coup* was masterminded by Colonel – .

In spite of this very limited correct usage of the dash, some people scatter dashes all through their letters, because their knowledge of the rules of punctuation is so weak that they cannot trust themselves to use the right mark in the right place. Whenever they feel a pause is needed they use a dash and hope for the best.

A business letter peppered with dashes does not look right, however, so it is well worth while to brush up on the rules if they are not clear in your mind. With sentences getting shorter and shorter, and commas being used less often, it is not really very hard to punctuate a letter correctly.

## Common abbreviations

Nowadays almost everything has its abbreviation and innumerable companies, bodies and organisations are known mainly by their initials. In the same way many people use qualifications after their names, and in certain cases other initials should follow a person's name on the envelope, as we shall see later in this chapter.

Meanwhile, here are some of the abbreviations commonly used in business:

**aar** against all risks
**a.c.** alternating current
**a/c** account or account current
**acct** account
**ack.** acknowledge/d
**A.D.** *or* **a.d.** after date
**Add.** addenda/addendum
**A/o** account of
**A/r** all risks
**B/E** bill of entry/bill of exchange
**B/F** *or* **b/f** brought forward
**b/g** bonded goods
**B/H** bill of health

**bhp** brake horsepower
**B/L** bill of lading
**bl** bale/barrel
**bo** buyer's option
**b/o** brought over
**B/p** bill of parcels/bills payable
**°C** degrees centigrade (or Celsius)
**C/A** credit or current account
**c&d** collection and delivery
**C&F** cost and freight
**cf** compare

**CIF** *or* **cif**   cost, insurance, freight
**C/o**   care of/carried over/cash order
**COD**   cash on delivery
**collat.**   collateral
**cp**   compare
**c/r**   company's risk
**c.v.d.**   cash against documents
**cwo**   cash with order
**D/a**   deposit account
**d/a**   days after acceptance
**dbk**   drawback
**deb**   debenture/debit
**dely**   delivery
**d/f**   dead freight
**d/o**   delivery order
**doc/s**   document/s
**doz.**   dozen
**D/p**   documents against payment
**D/R**   deposit receipt
**D/S**   day's sight/days after sight
**EEC**   European Economic Community
**e.g.**   *exempli gratia* (for example)
**E&OE**   Errors and omissions excepted
**enc.**   enclosure/s
**°F**   degrees Fahrenheit
**f&d**   freight and demurrage
**FAS** *or* **fas**   free alongside steamer
**F/d**   free docks
**fd**   forward
**ffa**   free from alongside
**FOB** *or* **fob**   free on board
**frt**   freight
**frt/fwd**   freight forward
**frt/ppd**   freight prepaid

**g**   gram(me)
**gr. wt.**   gross weight
**HMSO**   Her Majesty's Stationery Office
**i.e.**   *id est* (that is)
**kg**   kilogram(me)
**km**   kilometre
**l**   litre
**L/C**   letter of credit
**LIFO**   last in first out
**LILO**   last in last out
**m**   metre
**MD**   Managing Director
**mm**   millimetre
**N.B.**   *Nota bene* (note well)
**n/m**   no mark
**n/p**   net proceeds
**n.t.**   net tonnage
**o/d**   on demand
**o.n.o.**   or nearest offer
**opn**   opinion/option
**o/s**   on sale (or return)
**P/A**   private account
**p.a.**   *per annum* (yearly)
**PAYE**   Pay As You Earn
**PCB**   petty cash book
**per pro** *or* **p.p.**   *per procurationem* (with the authority of)
**pd**   paid/port dues
**p/d**   post dated
**P/N**   promissory note
**ppd**   post paid/prepaid
**RSVP**   *Répondez s'il vous plaît* (please reply)
**s.a.e.**   stamped addressed envelope
**so**   seller's option
**viz.**   *videlicet* (namely)
**wt**   weight
**xd**   ex dividend

# The business letter

Most business letters have a threefold aim:

1 To transmit a message from writer to recipient.
2 To move the recipient to action.
3 To imbue the recipient with friendly feelings towards the writer and his company.

If you follow the rule of brevity and simplicity you should go a long way towards achieving the first and second aims. The third aim calls for a courteous and friendly tone at all times. As you know, it is possible to say 'no' in a courteous way. Conversely, however much money a customer might owe the company, asking for it in a discourteous way will not make it any easier for you to recover it. So always use a courteous tone in your letters and do not allow brevity to become curtness.

Before you write a letter, establish clearly in your own mind the message you wish to convey, and gather together the information you need for the purpose. You might need to look up another file, make a phone call, read some papers or consult someone else. When all your information is before you, jot down the points you want to make before you begin.

When you finally get down to writing, make your first point, then immediately move on to the next one. Resist the temptation to elaborate needlessly. So many people make the same point over and over again, first in one way, then in another. Try to think of the best possible way of saying what you mean, and leave it at that.

If you are replying to a letter which asks several questions, reply to each one in the same order. Do not leave any question unanswered, as nothing is more irritating to a correspondent.

## Layout

There are various accepted ways of laying out a business letter. The most up-to-date way is to block everything to the left, without any indentations at all. Even the complimentary close and the signature will be flush left (see Fig. 5.1).

The semi-blocked layout consists of indenting every fresh paragraph, usually five spaces. The complimentary close, the name of the company and the name and designation of the sender are indented (see Fig. 5.2). This type of layout is still quite common.

Bloggs, Bloggs, and Bloggs,
Architects,
25, Lincoln Street,
LONDON W1 2QX.
Telephone: 01.232.2461
Telex: 285603
Registered No. 1037295

Your Ref: Op 6

Our Ref: PR/abb

23 October 19_ _

Miss M Bosticco
15 The Avenue
SOMETOWN
Buckinghamshire
SL8 5TY


Dear Miss Bosticco

Thank you for your letter dated 10 October
expressing your interest in our new letter-
headings.

We too think that they are rather smart, and
agree with you that nothing could be more
important than the design and layout of a
letter, since a letter is frequently the very
first sight of a firm's image which a potential
client gets.

By all means use our letter-heading in your
new book, indeed we feel rather proud to have
been asked.

If you need any further assistance, do let
us know.

Yours sincerely

*AB Bloggs*

A B Bloggs   Senior Partner

**Fig. 5.1**   A fully-blocked letter

Bloggs, Bloggs, and Bloggs,
Architects,
25, Lincoln Street,
LONDON W1 2QX.
Telephone: 01.232.2461
Telex: 285603
Registered No. 1037295

Your Ref: Op 6

Our Ref: PR/abb

23 October 19_ _

Miss M Bosticco
15 The Avenue
SOMETOWN
Buckinghamshire
SL8 5TY

Dear Miss Bosticco,

    Thank you for your letter dated 10 October
expressing your interest in our new letter-
headings.

    We too think that they are rather smart,
and agree with you that nothing could be more
important than the design and layout of a
letter, since a letter is frequently the very
first sight of a firm's image which a potential
client gets.

    By all means use our letter-heading in
your new book, indeed we feel rather proud to
have been asked.

    If you need any further assistance, do
let us know.

                    Yours sincerely,

                    A B Bloggs

                    A B Bloggs
                    Senior Partner

**Fig. 5.2** A semi-blocked letter

Many organisations provide their secretaries and typists with detailed instructions on how to lay out the company's letters. In such cases, you have only to follow instructions.

**The date**

The usual form in Britain is:

23rd March 1984

Some organisations omit the *th*, *nd* or *rd*, while American companies prefer March 23, 1984. Where figures alone are used, the British custom is to give first the day, then the month, and then the year, e.g. 23/3/1984. In the USA the month is shown first, followed by the day, exactly as is done when the date is written out in full, e.g. 3/23/1984.

**The reference**

It is extremely important to include both the addressee's and your own company's references in all letters, as it saves a great deal of time in locating past correspondence on the same subject and also ensures that your letter quickly reaches the desk of the person for whom it is intended. The kind of reference you use will depend on your company's filing system. If it is quite a small organisation your reference may simply be 'Adv.' or 'Exp.', according to the department, followed by the dictator's initials and your own. If you have devised your own filing system you will know best how to identify the letters you send out. Whatever the circumstances, however, never send out a letter without a reference of some sort. If you have nothing else to go by, then simply put the dictator's initials followed by your own. This at least ensures that any reply will reach the right person.

Most business letterheads have the words 'Your Ref.' and 'Our Ref.' already printed on them. If this is not the case, type them in, always quoting the other company's reference first. Some companies do not type references, but have them printed in pairs on tiny gummed labels which are fixed to outgoing mail. The recipient then detaches half of the label and attaches it to his reply.

**The addressee**

Strictly speaking, every business letter should be addressed to the company or organisation for which it is intended. It should begin

'Dear Sirs', and end 'Yours faithfully'. Nowadays, however, it is customary for businessmen to write to each other as individuals, addressing their letters to: Mr W. H. Brown, followed by the name of the company and the address, including the post code. The letter begins 'Dear Mr Brown' or 'Dear Bill' and ends 'Yours sincerely'. Some companies and the Civil Service still use 'Esq.' The form of address would then be W. H. Brown, Esq.

When women sign their letters they may indicate, in brackets after their surname, whether they wish to be addressed as 'Mrs', Miss' or 'Ms'. If they give no indication, then you should use 'Ms'.

A business letter can be addressed to the company, but with 'Att: Mr W. H. Brown' either centred or blocked left, according to your layout. If you use this form, then the letter should open 'Dear Sirs', since it is addressed to the company.

If you are writing to a company or organisation for the first time and do not know the name of the executive you want, address your letter to him by title, e.g. 'The Sales Manager' or 'The Company Secretary'. Otherwise the letter may easily be delayed, especially if written to a large organisation.

If you are writing to a partnership, the correct form of address is: 'Messrs Swift, Green, and Golding' or 'Messrs W. F. Brown and G. W. Wright', as indicated on their letterhead. In the case of a limited company or other corporate body it is, strictly speaking, incorrect to use 'Messrs', although many companies do so.

Some executives like to handwrite the 'Dear Mr So-and-So', the 'Dear Ms Bloggs' or the 'Dear Bill', as well as the complimentary close. If your chief prefers to do this, leave plenty of space, since handwriting often takes up more room than typewriting and the letter looks better if the handwritten bits are not cramped.

However you address your letter – and the choice will seldom be yours – always make absolutely certain you have the correct spelling. Almost everyone feels very strongly about the spelling of their own name and some people are quite put out if their name is incorrectly spelled. The same care should be taken in getting a person's title, rank or qualification letters right. Correct forms of address are dealt with later in this chapter.

If you do not know the addressee's correct forename or initials, look them up in previous correspondence or, as a last resort, telephone and ask his secretary. It is not good form to address a letter simply to 'Mr Brown' or 'Miss Brown'.

If you are writing to a foreign firm, write the full name of the company as it is given on their letterhead and precede it with the following:

German companies: *Firma*
French companies: *MM*
Italian companies: *Spett. Ditta*
Spanish and Latin American companies: *Sres*

However, as with English forms of address, there is more to it than this – for instance a French *Société Anonyme* is addressed simply as *Soc. An.* without a preceding *MM*. All correspondence with companies abroad should be conducted in the appropriate language whenever possible, although English is widely used.

Letters containing confidential information should be marked CONFIDENTIAL, in capital letters and preferably in red, immediately above the address, and again on the envelope. Letters containing information of a private and personal nature, such as matters concerning salary, leave of absence, and so on, should be marked PERSONAL, again in capital letters and preferably in red or other distinctive colour. Do not mark a letter PERSONAL when you mean CONFIDENTIAL. There is a very distinct difference: only the addressee should deal with personal affairs, while a deputy can deal with confidential matters.

### The letter opening

We have already dealt with how business letters should begin, and a later section covers special forms of address. Your opening should always be consistent with the way in which the letter is addressed, as well as with the salutation or complimentary close. If, for instance, your letter is addressed to a company, organisation or partnership, then it should begin 'Dear Sirs', in the plural. If, on the other hand, it is addressed to 'The Sales Manager, Joseph White Plc,' then it should begin 'Dear Sir'. Both letters should end 'Yours faithfully'. American companies would begin a letter addressed to a company with 'Gentlemen', and end it with 'Yours truly'. If addressed to the Sales Manager, as in the second example, an American company would begin the letter 'Dear Sir' and end it 'Yours truly'.

Women should be addressed formally as 'Dear Madam' and less formally as 'Dear Mrs Jones', 'Dear Miss Smith' or 'Dear Ms Brown', as explained previously. If you have to address a body of two or more women, then the correct form is 'Mesdames', without the 'Dear'.

If the letter is addressed to a person by name, then it should begin 'Dear Mr (or Miss) Brown' and end 'Your sincerely', unless of course you have been instructed to write 'Dear Bill', in which case the letter should still end 'Yours sincerely'.

Whatever form of address you adopt, never use a formal opening with an informal close or vice versa. This means, quite simply, that if you begin 'Dear Sir', 'Dear Sirs' or 'Dear Madam', then you must perforce end with 'Yours faithfully' and never with 'Yours sincerely'. If the chief has written in the 'Dear So-and-So' by hand, don't forget to type it in on the carbon so you have a record of what was done.

### The body of the letter

Almost every business letter should begin by stating its object. This can be in the form of a heading, either centred or flush left, immediately under the 'Dear Sirs'. Even if it has not been dictated, there is no reason why you should not begin your letter by briefly stating what it is about. It is an excellent practice because it helps the recipient to see the main theme at a glance, and it also makes filing easier for both parties. It is also good practice to write a separate letter for each subject, as this may save hours searching for a letter in the files only to discover that it was filed under the second subject with which it dealt. Here again is something you can do on your own initiative whenever you are given an outline for a letter dealing with two or more subjects. If it does not prove possible to write separate letters, then be sure to make separate carbons for each subject so they can be filed in their respective folders and cross-referenced.

There is no need to preface a subject reference with 'Ref.', 'Re:' or 'Obj.', since it is quite obvious to all what the heading is about.

### The close

We have already seen how you should end your letter and special cases are given later in this chapter. All that is strictly necessary after the 'Yours faithfully' is a space for the signature and the name of the sender with his title or designation underneath. This is the most up-to-date way of doing it. It is simple, practical and correct. The recipient of the letter will know perfectly well which company or organisation it is from, since he has it on the letterhead. However, most companies have their own ideas on how they want their letters to conclude and you will obviously have to follow instructions on this point.

If you write letters in your own name, use the following form:

Judith Collins (Miss)
Secretary to W. J. Wilson
Sales Manager

If the chief dictates some letters and plans to be away before they are typed, make sure you ask him if, and how, he would like you to sign them. If they are important letters which commit the company in some way, he will want them to wait until his return or he will arrange for another company executive to sign them on his behalf. If it is simply a routine letter, he may ask you to use the form: 'Dictated by Mr Wilson and signed in his absence' and you will then sign the letter, using your own name. In fact you should never sign another person's name: it could get you into serious trouble. If you have been specifically authorised to do so, you may write 'p.p.' or 'per pro' ('with the authority of') alongside the chief's name when you sign the letter. Alternatively you can use the word 'for'

**Enclosures**
If your letter is to have one or more enclosures, you should indicate this fact at the foot of the letter. The usual form is to write 'Encl.', 'Enclosure' or 'Enclosures 2'. Some companies use small gummed labels printed ENCLOSURE. One is affixed at the foot of the letter and the other on the enclosure itself. Another method, used in government departments, is to type a line or three dashes in the margin alongside the mention of an enclosure. If you mention a catalogue or other item which is to follow separately, it is helpful if you indicate this at the foot of the letter. For example, say 'Sample follows by parcel post'. This enables the person receiving the letter to watch out for the separate parcel or envelope and, at the same time, it is a useful reminder for your files.

**The envelope**

If your company uses window envelopes you will be saved a great deal of work and nothing need be said about the typing of envelopes. Otherwise, the block form is almost universally adopted. Obviously, the address on the envelope should exactly match the one on the letter, and any indication such as PRIVATE, CONFIDENTIAL or BY HAND should go on the envelope too. The section which follows will give you some guidance on how to address people with titles, rank, qualifications or official status.

**Forms of address**

We have already seen how important it is to spell a person's name correctly, and to include the correct initials or forename. It is equally important to use the correct title, rank or degree. This can be more difficult than simply spelling the name correctly, since this kind of information is seldom given on incoming letters.

Letters denoting Masters' or Bachelors' degrees, such as M.A., B.A. and B.Sc., are rarely used, except when writing to someone in the teaching profession. Letters indicating professional qualifications or official status should be used only for professional or official correspondence. One exception to this rule is M.P., which should always follow the name of a Member of Parliament. The other exception is Q.C. (Queen's Counsel), which should also always be used.

Physicians and surgeons are correctly addressed simply as 'Esq', followed by their qualification letters. However, it is perfectly in order to address a letter to a physician: Dr W. F. Jones, since 'Doctor' is a courtesy title generally given to a physician, whether he has the corresponding degree or not.

Letters to clergymen are addressed: To the Rev. George White. Officers in the armed forces are addressed according to rank, giving the full forename or initials, followed by the surname. For instance: Lieutenant-General B. F. Watson; Air Commodore J. J. Bliss, RAF; Group Officer Joan Wright, WRAF.

For a complete list of forms of address, including the peerage, one of the most useful reference books is *Titles and Forms of Address, A Guide to Their Correct Use*, published by A. & C. Black, London. Other reference books are listed in the Appendix.

## The internal memorandum

A memorandum, or memo as it is usually called, is quite simply a letter to another department or another company branch. As such it does not require elaborate addressing, neither does it need to be written on expensive paper or to be couched in formal terms. It may, indeed, be handwritten.

Most organisations supply memo paper or pads, pre-printed with the heading 'Memorandum' and underneath: To, From, Date, Ref., Subject. If your company does not do so, simply type out such a heading on a plain sheet of paper.

Memos can be written quite informally, thereby fostering inter-personal relations between the different members of staff. Many organisations, however, ignore this potential bonus and use a very cold impersonal style in their memos, frequently addressing them by function instead of by name. Obviously, in this matter, as in most others, you will have to follow instructions.

Memos do not usually have a formal salutation at the beginning or at the end and are not usually signed with the sender's full name, but with initials only (see Fig. 5.3).

## The report

A report is a formal account of an investigation into a given subject. Above all, a report must be accurate, clearly arranged, simple and easy to read. One cannot lay down hard and fast rules for the writing of all reports, but the following outline can be used in the majority of cases:

1   Begin with a *heading* or title, clearly indicating what the report is about. Then state to whom it is addressed, and from whom it is sent. Give the date and a reference number for future identification.

2   Then indicate the *terms of reference* of your report. This should simply answer the question of why you are writing the report. At its simplest it could mean writing: 'As you requested, I have carried out an investigation on the number of hours wasted in the office by private telephone calls.'

3   Next you should indicate the *method of investigation* or pro-cedure employed. This section of your report could include several numbered paragraphs detailing the action taken.

**MEMORANDUM**

**To:** All members of staff

**From:** Office Manager

**Date:** 7 November 198–

**Ref:** MB/GGS

CHRISTMAS HOLIDAYS

Since Christmas Day falls on a Sunday this year, the Managing Director has decided that the Company will close down from the afternoon of Friday, 23 December, at the usual time of 5.30 p.m., until the morning of Wednesday, 28 December at 9 a.m.

**Fig. 5.3** A memorandum

4   *Findings*. Your fourth step is to give the result of your investigations. What facts did you uncover? What did you find?

5   *Recommendations*. Sometimes your initial terms of reference will include making recommendations. In such cases you will go on to recommend the action you believe to be required as a result of your findings.

6   The report usually ends with the signature and position of the person who carried out the investigation, and the date, unless the latter has already been given at the head of the report.

As a secretary, your main contribution to writing reports will probably consist of putting someone else's notes into readable form. Knowing the ground rules will help you a great deal with this task. However, you may well have occasion to write a report of your own, and Fig. 5.4 shows a report written by a secretary who has been asked to go to the Business Efficiency exhibition and report on any piece of equipment which might be useful in the office. As this is an internal report, it is rather like a memo.

## The circular letter

The circular letter is one which is sent out not to one person, but to hundreds or even thousands. Nowadays, with the advent of the word processor, each letter does not have to be identical, since this machine makes it possible to insert variations into every letter automatically, thereby giving the recipient the impression that it was written for him alone.

Once written, the letters are duplicated in one of a number of ways and sent to their destination. The master letter can be stored by the word processor to be re-used later, probably with further amendments.

The classical example of the circular letter is the sales letter. You have probably received quite a few of them yourself, attempting to sell you books, wall plates, double glazing and so on. The writing of a sales letter is a specialised job. It cannot hope to succeed unless it is undertaken by someone who has first mastered the basic principles of salesmanship.

There are other kinds of circular letter, however, such as the ones sent out by the personnel department announcing closures for holidays, new rules and regulations, and so on. This type of letter is

To:  Mr John Jones                    From: Mary Green
     Managing Director                23 March 198-

                      OFFICE EQUIPMENT

As you requested, I visited the Business Efficiency
Exhibition yesterday.

I spent half a day there and saw several machines
intended to automate and speed-up routine office
work.  However, I felt that most of them would be
more appropriate for companies larger than ours.

One machine which would be of great value in our
office is a word processor.  I spent some time at
one of the stands displaying this equipment and
tried out one of the machines.  I got the impression
that I could quickly learn to use it, and was told
that the company provides tuition and training for
new users.

Regular use of a word processor would:

1   Speed up the production of business correspon-
    dence.

2   Enable sales letters to be edited on the machine,
    and thus save time.

3   Enable us to store these letters for re-use later
    on, perhaps with further editing.

4   Enable us to store our mailing list, and address
    both letters and envelopes at the touch of a
    button.

I therefore recommend that we acquire a word processor as soon as possible.  Supporting literature
is attached.

                        *Mary Green*

**Fig. 5.4**   A specimen report

usually presented in memo form addressed to 'All Members of the Staff'.

The same basic letter can also be sent out to acknowledge orders, prompt customers to settle debts, and even to place orders. This type of basic letter is often called a 'form letter' and can be stored on the word processor or otherwise preserved for repeated use.

## Invitations

The invitation surely needs no formal definition. Both writing and replying to invitations are activities which all secretaries can expect to perform sometimes.

Invitations can be either formal or informal. The latter do not need special attention, since an informal invitation simply takes the form of a letter and should be answered accordingly. The formal invitation, on the other hand, has to follow a set formula, as shown in Fig. 5.5.

For business events the formula is modified as shown in Fig. 5.6.

```
                    Mr and Mrs John Cooper

                    request the pleasure of

                         the company of

                      Mr Frederick Allen

                          at dinner on

                      Friday, October 25

                       at eight o'clock


R.S.V.P.
'The Haven'
Cherry Lane
Chalfont St Peter
Buckinghamshire                                    Black tie
```

**Fig. 5.5**    A formal invitation

```
            The Chairman and Directors of

     The Wonder Company of Great Britain Plc

            request the pleasure of

                 the company of

               Mr Frederick Allen

     to the opening of their new headquarters

               at 224 Cannon Street

               on Friday, October 25

               at eleven o'clock

R.S.V.P.
Ms Jane Rich
Secretary to the Managing Director
The Wonder Company of Great Britain Plc
224 Cannon Street
LONDON
WC2 7FB                              Cocktails
```

**Fig. 5.6**   A business invitation

The formal invitation is usually engraved on a white card and the guest's name is written in by hand. Invitations should go out about three weeks before the event to give more people the opportunity of accepting. They should always specify the date, the time and the place of the event in question. In the case of business events, their exact nature should also be specified, and it is also useful to give an indication of whether there is to be food, drink, or both. In the case of evening events it is usual to specify the dress to be worn.

Invitations should be answered within two days to assist the hosts. If you were Ms Jane Rich of our example, however, you would soon learn that many businessmen not only fail to reply within two days, but do not reply at all, leaving you with the task of phoning around to ask whether they propose to accept your company's kind invitation.

```
                    Mr Frederick Allen

      has much pleasure in accepting the kind invitation of

                  Mr and Mrs John Cooper

                        to dinner

        on Friday, October 25 at eight o'clock
```

**Fig. 5.7**   A formal acceptance

A formal acceptance should be couched in exactly the same terms as the invitation itself. It should be centred, preferably on a letterheading, as shown in Fig. 5.7.

Nothing else should be added, but note that the date and time have been repeated. Replies to The Wonder Company of Great Britain should be similarly worded. If the invitation has to be turned down, the same rules apply.

## Telemessages and international telegrams

The traditional telegraph service, invaluable to business for over one hundred years, has all but passed into history. There is therefore no need to dwell on it at great length. It is reduced now to the *telemessage* and the *international telegram*.

*Telemessages* can be sent by telephone, public payphone or by Telex up to 8 p.m. from Monday to Saturday (or up to 9 p.m. from a London address) for delivery by post on the next working day. Telemessages arrive in bright yellow envelopes with blue lettering, and are used in business for quotations, specifications, instructions and sales promotions.

*International telegrams* are likewise sent by telephone or by Telex. Telegrams are a very expensive way of communicating, so in order to cut down the expense as much as possible, two devices were invented. One is the telegraphic address, which has to be registered, and the other is telegraphese. The telegraphic address consists of two words, one indicating the company, and the other the town. Companies print their telegraphic address on their letterheads, so that all their correspondents know it.

Telegraphese is the terse, pared-to-the bone language used to write telegrams. A telegram should not be written in a hurry, for it is only too easy to leave out some essential information in an attempt to be brief. So look at it carefully, make sure all essential information has been included, then cut out all unnecessary words. Punctuation is also omitted, the full stop being replaced by the word 'Stop'.

## The teleprinter and Telex

The teleprinter is a machine for typing messages to a distant place. Whatever you type on your machine, is typed out at the same time on the machine at the other end of the line. Telex is an exchange service like the telephone service, but uses teleprinters instead of telephones.

You can send messages to, and receive messages from, any other Telex subscriber in the UK, and most of those abroad. You simply dial the Telex number of the subscriber you want in Britain or in Europe, while for some other countries a combination of dialling and keying on the teleprinter keyboard are necessary. You have to ask the operator to connect you to subscribers any further afield.

The teleprinter has a keyboard very like a typewriter keyboard and, having dialled the appropriate subscriber's number and received the answerback code, you simply type your message as you would on a typewriter. In writing a Telex message, there are no hard and fast rules nor any particular complications. You should simply bear in mind that Telex messages are expensive to transmit, so that a terse style in preferable, though not quite so terse as telegraphese. More information on the teleprinter is given in Chapter 14.

## Visual telecommunications

A picture is worth a thousand words, an ancient Chinese proverb tells us. This saying seems to have been taken to heart during the second half of this century, which has seen a bewildering proliferation of visual aids penetrating homes and offices alike.

A whole book would be needed to describe all of them, so we shall simply describe the four aspects of visual telecommunications most likely to be encountered in the modern office.

**Viewdata**

Viewdata is a computer-based information service which works through the medium of a television set. There are three public systems in Britain at the moment: *Ceefax*, provided by the BBC; *Oracle*, provided by ITV; and *Prestel*, provided by British Telecom.

The first two systems, sometimes known as Teletext, are broadcast, whereas Prestel uses the telephone network to link the user of an adapted television set to 'pages' of information held on a computer.

All three services provide information on the weather, business and sports reports, and recreation. In fact, Prestel has over 200 000 'pages' of information to choose from, covering a range of topics, and the number increases daily.

Prestel is by far the most sophisticated system, which now extends

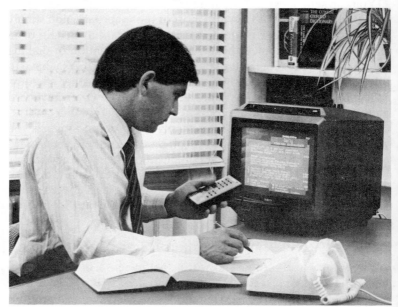

**Fig. 5.8**   A Prestel viewdata system

to many countries overseas, including the USA. Through Prestel you can gain access to other national viewdata systems and also to a wide range of non-viewdata computers.

Prestel is the only public viewdata system which you can 'talk back' to. This means that it is not merely possible to decide which typewriter is the best value for money, but also to order one by Prestel. You can also book airline tickets, reserve hotel rooms and send messages to other Prestel subscribers.

A Prestel television can be bought or rented from a television retailer or rental company. The set enables you to receive Prestel as well as the usual choice of television services. British Telecom then connects the television set to the telephone by way of a jack-plug. Purpose-built Prestel sets with an integral telephone are also available.

The Prestel television set is equipped with a remote control device which looks rather like a pocket calculator and is called a keypad. On it are a series of numbered buttons. By pressing one of the buttons you contact the Prestel computer via your telephone line. Prestel then announces itself with a cheery 'Welcome to Prestel' which appears on your television screen. At the press of a second button, an index of the available information appears. You then go on from there, summoning up the required information at the press of a button. Once accessed, information can also be recorded on cassette or print-outs, thereby cutting down the cost of using the Prestel telephone and computer link.

**Closed circuit television**

Closed circuit television is a means of providing visual communication between two or more points. It is probably best known to you as a surveillance system used by many department stores. It is also useful for conferences and training sessions, such as in interviewing technique.

**Confravision**

Confravision is a service which links individuals or groups of people in different cities by sound and vision. Users can conduct discussions, meetings and presentations between studios at distant locations as though they were face to face in the same room.

At the moment there are five studios in Britain. They are in

London, Bristol, Birmingham, Manchester and Glasgow. The sound-proof studios can accommodate five people seated at a conference table, with room for a further four behind. A row of push-buttons is located in front of the centre seat, and its user can control the camera range, the microphone and the tape recorder, which can be used either to record the conference or to transmit pre-recorded messages. A display camera is also provided to transmit black-and-white pictures of documents, graphs, charts, and small objects.

Confravision conferences can be set up between any two or three studios in Britain and also with studios in the Netherlands and in Sweden. There is no doubt that this facility is a useful one for businessmen who want to save travelling time and its inherent delays and inconvenience.

### Facsimile transmission

Facsimile transmission, as the name implies, is a means of transmitting documents by telephone. The Fax machines can be bought or rented from a number of suppliers or from British Telecom. The latter then connects the machine to the telephone line and it is ready for use. You can then transmit drawings, diagrams, layouts and documents in three minutes or less, regardless of distance.

The advantages of such machines are obvious. The only disadvantage at the moment is that your documents can be received only by someone with a compatible machine. However, work is underway to make facsimile machines all over the world compatible with each other.

Meanwhile, a good way of avoiding the problem of machine compatibility is to use British Telecom's Bureaufax. This is a service for forwarding documents overseas via facsimile transmission. It is obviously also useful if a company does not have a Fax machine of its own.

Documents to be 'faxed' are simply handed in over the counter at one of the many acceptance offices in England, Scotland or Wales. They can be sent by post to the same offices or they can be sent via your own facsimile machine. Documents can also be received from abroad via Bureaufax, and thence via your own facsimile machine or first-class post.

**Questions**

1 Your employer, the Sales Executive of a Shoe Company, has asked you to write to several hotels in the district enquiring if they can accommodate fifty people for a one-day conference from 0930 to 1730 hours next November. Prices for morning coffee, luncheon and afternoon tea will also be required. Write this letter for your employer's approval, including all he has requested and asking for any other information you feel may be necessary. (Pitman Secretarial Practice Intermediate.)

2 In the past few months it has been necessary for a mechanic to repair frequently various electrical appliances in your office. On his last visit it was intimated that the faults were the result of misuse by staff. Your employer asks you to prepare a memorandum to staff, drawing their attention to this state of affairs, and giving them a set of rules for the care of machines to avoid so many breakdowns. Write this memorandum. (Pitman Secretarial Practice Intermediate.)

3 Your employer has received a formal invitation to a business dinner, and the letters RSVP are printed on the bottom corner. What does this indicate you should do? (Pitman Secretarial Practice Intermediate.)

4 During the last Departmental meeting there was a request for a simple and economic method which would assist the mail room in distinguishing between copies of correspondence intended for distribution to different sections of the warehouse and factory. All typists use electric typewriters. Mr Watson, your employer, has asked you to suggest an inexpensive way of dealing with this problem and one that will be easily handled by the mailroom. Provide a report explaining how this could be done and what necessary action you will suggest to Mr Watson for such a solution to be carried out. (RSA Secretarial Duties Stage II.)

5 Circular letters are used for a number of purposes. Give two of them.

6 Write, on your employer's behalf, accepting the invitation from The Wonder Company of Great Britain Plc, given on p. 79.

7 Answer the following questions:
   (*a*) What is Viewdata and what is it used for?
   (*b*) Which are the three public systems of visual communication at present provided in the UK, and who provides them?

8  In what circumstances would you use the following methods of communication:
   (*a*)  Telephone
   (*b*)  Telex
   (*c*)  Facsimile transmission
9  You work for a company based in London, with branches in Bristol, Birmingham and Glasgow. Your chief spends much of his time travelling between these four points. He could actually hold a conference with his three branch managers without moving from his office, and be able to see them and talk to them as if they were present. What service would he have to use to do this? Give details of this service.

# 6

# Stationery and Stock Control

## Sizes of paper

Business letters are usually written on headed paper which conforms to international paper sizes laid down by the International Standards Organisation. These ISO sizes come in three series: A, B and C. The A series is used for stationery and printed leaflets; B is mainly for larger printed matter, such as posters; and C is for envelopes, to be used in conjunction with the A-sized stationery.

The A series is based on a master sheet, the A0 sheet, which measures exactly one square metre. By folding the A0 sheet in half, we arrive at the A1 size, measuring 594 mm × 841 mm. By folding the A1 sheet in half we have the A2 size, and so on until we have the A7 sheet measuring 74 mm × 105 mm. The two sizes in most common use for business letters are A4, measuring 210 mm × 297 mm, and A5 for shorter letters.

There are many advantages in using ISO paper sizes, but the two main ones for you to bear in mind are that: (*a*) since most countries use the ISO sizes, standardisation means easier filing; and (*b*) the Post Office's sorting task is speeded up, as electronic sorting equipment can be used at maximum efficiency.

Unfortunately, however, the International Standards Organisation and the Universal Postal Union have obviously not been working hand-in-hand, and the Post Office has adopted preferred envelope sizes of its own. Post Office Preferred (POP) envelopes should measure at least 90 mm ×140 mm and be no larger than 120 mm × 235 mm. They should be oblong in shape, with the longer side at least 1·414 times the shorter side and they should be made from paper weighing at least 63 grams per square metre. Only the ISO size C6 comes within the POP range. Moreover, the most popular commercial envelope – the DL size for A4 letters – is also outside the C series, although it conforms to Post Office requirements. The DL size was thought up by the Germans, who originated the idea of a series of standard paper sizes.

POP sizes apply only to letters weighing up to 60 g, and the Post Office has the power to make additional charges for letters and cards which do not conform. So far, however, they have not exercised these powers.

## Grades of paper

The grades of paper generally used in the office are:

1  *Bond*  This is a high quality, durable paper, available in a number of weights. It is suitable for letter-headings, compliment slips, continuation sheets and, in a lighter weight, for internal memoranda.

2  *Bank*  This is often called 'flimsy' and it is, in fact, flimsier than bond, but still of durable quality. It is suitable for carbon copies.

3  *Duplicating paper*  A semi-absorbent paper is required for ink duplicating processes, and a calendered paper for spirit duplicating.

4  *Carbon paper*  This is available in a number of weights, according to the number of copies it can produce: the lighter the weight, the more copies can be produced at a single impression, although the heavier weights will last longer. The five grades are:

|  | *Number of copies* |
|---|---|
| Super heavyweight | 1 – 2 |
| Heavyweight | 1 – 3 |
| Standard weight | 4 – 6 |
| Manifold | 7 – 10 |
| Supermanifold | 11 – 15 |

Do bear in mind, however, that when you need many copies you should also use thinner typing paper.

Good quality carbon paper can be used over and over again, up to about forty times, especially if you turn the sheets around to distribute the wear. You should treat it kindly, however, laying it face downwards, away from heat and without creasing it. *Copying film* is more expensive than carbon paper, but lasts much longer, producing up to two hundred copies from each sheet.

All carbon papers are available in a number of colours and usually have a cut corner, a protruding tab or extra length for easy withdrawal from the paper sheets.

## The stationery cupboard

Apart from the various grades of paper, your stationery cupboard will contain most of the following:

**Envelopes** We have already discussed sizes. Envelopes are also available in a number of grades and types. For correspondence a good quality bond envelope is generally used, sometimes with the company's name and address on the front. *Window* envelopes have a cut-out panel covered with transparent material through which the address on the document can be read. These envelopes obviously save time since the address only has to be typed once. The Post Office has nothing against them, providing they are in POP sizes. *Aperture* envelopes are similar to window envelopes, but without the transparent cover over the cut-out panel. The Post Office objects to these even if they are in POP sizes. *Padded* envelopes are very useful for mailing books, diaries, or any small item which needs protection en route. The Post Office sells a range of them in various sizes, and they are also available from stationers. *Plastic* envelopes are frequently used for mailing magazines or other printed matter. *Manilla* envelopes are extra-strong envelopes, available in a number of sizes, which are used for letters containing several enclosures or to mail any bulky material, including catalogues. Some of these envelopes are supplied with metal fastening clips, and some of them have ungummed flaps, which are tucked in when mailing something abroad at the printed paper rate. Cardboard-reinforced manilla envelopes are also available. *Internal* envelopes are reusable envelopes designed for the internal mail.

**Multi-set forms** We have already described these sets in Chapter 1. Each form in a set has the same serial number, but may be in a different colour with a different heading. The forms described in

Chapter 1 were headed 'Invoice', 'Delivery Note', 'File Copy', 'Accounts Copy' and so on, so that when they are typed they can be sent to their destination speedily and accurately. Multi-set forms may also be used for memos requiring a reply (for which there is space on the form) as well as for cheque requisitions, expenses forms and the like.

Thin 'one-time' carbon paper may be interleaved in the sets or NCR ('No carbon required') paper may be used. This is less messy and saves time.

**Continuous stationery**   The multi-set forms can be produced in a continuous length, with perforations between each set. In this way documents can be typed one after the other, without having to stop to insert and remove each set. Continuous stationery is stored in rolls or folded concertina-fashion.

**Memo pads**   As we saw in the last chapter, some companies have their memo forms made up into pads, joined at the top, like multi-set forms.

**Compliment slips**   These are usually replicas of the company's letter-heading, guillotined off at the top, and with the words 'With Compliments' added. They can be used to accompany a catalogue or any other item which has been requested and obviate the need to write a covering letter. The executive sending the item sometimes signs the compliment slips and adds a short message if he so wishes.

**Postcards**   Many companies use headed postcards with a standard message printed on them, usually acknowledging receipt of an order, a request, or perhaps a manuscript in the case of publishers.

To complete your array of consumable office supplies, as they are called officially, you will have most of the following items: adhesive labels for use on parcels and packages, adhesive tape, blotting paper, paper clips and bulldog clips; some kind of glue or gum; shorthand notebooks, or tapes, if everyone uses dictating equipment; correcting fluid or obliterating strips for the typists, unless everyone is lucky enough to use self-correcting electronic equipment; typewriter ribbons, pens, pencils, duplicator supplies, telephone message pads, files and folders, brown wrapping paper, elastic bands, scissors, staplers, staples and string.

# Stock control

If you are a secretary in a small company, it is quite likely that you will be asked to take over the control and ordering of stationery and other office supplies. It is quite conceivable that until you arrived on the scene everyone helped themselves to supplies from the cupboard and reordering was a haphazard affair.

Faced with such a situation, you will need first of all to take stock of what supplies you have, and store them neatly in the cupboard. Reams of paper are usually labelled, but if not, mark them clearly with a felt-tipped pen.

You will then need to set up a procedure for issuing stationery and to make sure that everyone knows what it is. You may decide to issue it on one morning a week and you will issue it only on presentation of a stationery requisition slip. You could easily make up and duplicate some of these slips yourself (see Fig. 6.1).

If you keep these requisitions by you, you will find them helpful when reordering, since by analysing them you will be able to see what quantities of each item are used within a certain period of time. This will help you to decide on the maximum and minimum stocks to be held.

```
                    STATIONERY REQUISITION


        Item            Quantity         Department

        ...........     ...........      ...........

        ...........     ...........      ...........

        ...........     ...........      ...........


        Date: ........  Signature:  ...............
```

**Fig. 6.1**  A stationery requisition slip

Set aside a fixed day each month to check your stock, and re-order when necessary. If you have fixed maximum and minimum quantities, when stock has fallen to its minimum level the quantity to re-order is easily decided by subtracting the minimum quantity from the maximum. The balance is the quantity to re-order.

One way to keep track of stocks is to keep a record card for each item of stationery (see Fig. 6.2). As you will see, it gives maximum and minimum stock levels, and records every movement inwards and outwards. In this way you can always see the stock level at a glance.

Your printed stationery will be ordered from your usual company supplier, but it is wise to keep the names of several suppliers by you and to compare both prices and performance. It pays to lend an ear and accept the free samples offered by visiting sales representatives who call, as this acquaints you with new products on the market, and may well lead to the discovery of a better supplier. So look, listen and try out, but in the final analysis make your own recommendation to the chief.

Finally, all companies go in for stocktaking at least once a year and this will include the stationery cupboard. Stocktaking is necess-

                         STOCK RECORD CARD

                        A4 letterhead paper

    Minimum level:10 reams    Maximum level:50 reams

    Date   Quantity    Supplier   Quantity   Dept   Balance
           Received               Issued

    .....  ........    ........   ........   .....  .......

    .....  ........    ........   ........   .....  .......

    .....  ........    ........   ........   .....  .......

    .....  ........    ........   ........   .....  .......

Fig. 6.2   A stock record card

ary not only to provide a check on the stock-keeping, but also in order to evaluate the stock itself for inclusion in the company's accounts. Large companies often have continuous stocktaking by computer, but in such cases you will be out of the picture and, indeed, will be relieved of stationery stock-keeping altogether.

**Questions**
1  Having recently taken over the ordering of stationery, what type of paper will you order to use for carbon copies?     (Pitman Secretarial Practice Intermediate.)
2  You are secretary to the Purchasing Manager and he has now asked you to accept responsibility for purchasing and controlling all items of stationery used in your company. How would you ensure that stock levels are maintained and what system would you use to control the issuing of stock to various departments? Include in your answer illustrations of any forms/cards you may use to achieve this.     (Pitman Secretarial Practice Intermediate.)
3  What are the two main advantages of using ISO paper sizes?
4  What is NCR paper?
5  List four types of envelope and their uses.
6  What is stocktaking, and why is it necessary?

# 7

# On the Telephone

The telephone is not only an invaluable means of communication. To those at the other end of the line it represents the voice of your company. What kind of voice will it be, flustered or monotonous, curt to the point of rudeness or interminably longwinded? Or will it be a cheerful and courteous voice, brisk without being curt, friendly but not familiar, always helpful and considerate?

The answer depends on you, and indeed on everyone in the company who uses the telephone. It is quite wrong to take the attitude that 'the way *I* behave on the telephone couldn't possibly make any difference': it *does*. Few things are as important for the secretary as the skilful and considerate use of the telephone.

If you can arrange to have the telephone, or telephones, on the left-hand side of your desk, so much the better. This leaves the right hand free to take notes. (Obviously, the reverse applies if you are left-handed.) Have a note pad and pencil always by the instrument, ready for action at any time.

## Speaking on the telephone

Bear in mind that when speaking on the telephone your voice alone has the task of conveying to the listener your attitude and personality, since he cannot see your expression. However, your voice always *does* convey these things quite accurately, so it pays to cultivate a cheerful and friendly tone. Always be courteous, however busy you may be, or however irritating the caller. Enjoy the satisfaction of knowing that if you remain courteous and helpful while the other person is being rude or losing his temper, you have the upper hand by demonstrating greater self-control and wisdom.

Do not speak in a dull monotone. Avoid this by modulating the voice – that is, by changing its pitch. One way to practise this is to start a new sentence in a low pitch, let it rise naturally (as it usually will of its own accord), and then bring it down again in your next sentence. A high-pitched voice is, of course, as bad as a low monotone, so if your voice is naturally high-pitched watch this point carefully. Bear in mind that a voice that rises higher and higher as the speaker becomes involved tends to sound hysterical at the other end.

Try not to sound hurried, flustered or impatient, for nothing is more disconcerting to the caller. It is a fallacy to believe that sounding hurried gives the impression of being busy; it is rather a sign of disorganisation and lack of control. Neither can you deceive yourself into believing that you will not sound hurried if you *do* feel harassed, for the feeling comes across unmistakably. So practise a relaxed, calm, unhurried tone of voice. It is perfectly possible to be brief without conveying haste and impatience. Try to be relaxed without being languid; brief without being curt.

Speak clearly, spelling out place names or other difficult words. Avoid colloquial expressions such as 'Hang on', 'Half a tick', and so on, and never, *never* call people 'love' or 'dear', not even the telephone operator. It might not be the telephone operator, after all, and executives do not like to be asked to 'Hold on, dear'.

If your caller cannot hear you, speak more distinctly, not more loudly. If you have a bad line, it helps to cup your hand around the mouthpiece. If you want to make an aside to someone else in the office or summon someone who just happens to be passing, cover up the mouthpiece before doing so. Nothing sounds more un-businesslike than the stage whisper of 'Fred, it's for you'.

Finally, listen attentively to what the caller is saying. If the message is a long one, it is quite easy to let your attention wander, sometimes with disastrous results. Learn to listen carefully. You may well be surprised at how much you pick up – far more than the words alone convey.

## The telephone in the electronic age

A veritable revolution is now in progress in the British telecommunications field. It is both a technological revolution and an opening up of the field to companies other than British Telecom. This double event is resulting in astonishing new developments, a new range of services, some of them quite awe-inspiring, and a healthy element of competition. A company is now free to install a British Telecom switchboard or one from another company, and to buy a telephone set from one of several sources. This competition gives the customer greater choice and keeps suppliers constantly on their toes to produce better equipment at more competitive prices.

System X, the all-electronic telephone exchange, is gradually being installed all over Britain. It is a digital system, employing solid-state micro-chip technology. The ultimate result of this changeover is that a number of services, including Telex, data, facsimile, electronic fund transfer and electronic mail will be carried over the same transmission paths as telephone calls. We shall then have a true Integrated Services Digital Network (ISDN).

This state of affairs is still some distance away, however. Meanwhile, Mercury Communications, British Telecom's new rival, is busily installing a nationwide digital network of its own. While the work is underway, it has launched its new service by using cellular microwave radio on a temporary basis. The new service is now operational in the City and West End of London. Birmingham and Manchester are next on the list, and a satellite link with North America is planned.

Telephone systems capable of redirecting calls to other extensions when the first one is engaged are already with us. There are also telephones which remember an engaged number and try it again, on request, until it is free.

A call connect system obviates the need for a telephone operator. It consists of a neat desk unit with a handset and keypad – no dial. Each extension has its own unit from which both external and internal calls can be made. Numbers are not dialled, but obtained by pressing the appropriate buttons on the key-pad.

More traditionally, outside calls are made through a switchboard and internal calls through the internal telephone system. This system is also being brought up to date, with key-pads rapidly

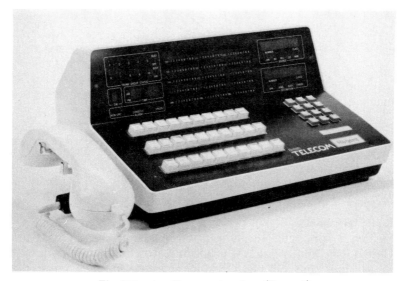

**Fig. 7.1** A call connect system (Regent)

replacing the traditional dial. Other refinements are also being added, such as conference facilities enabling up to six participants to confer at one time.

Another refinement, which is by no means new, is the loudspeaking telephone, which enables calls to be made or answered, both externally or internally, without the need to hold the handset. Apart from leaving the telephone-user's hands free, this device allows several people to be in on a call at the same time, and if the telephone operator is unable to locate the person wanted, but knows he is in the building, he can be called on the loudspeaker. If the person is out of the office, even hundreds of miles away, he can be called by means of a high-frequency radio paging system. The user carries a receiver, usually in his pocket, and when he is wanted he is alerted by a bleep. He then presses a button to receive the message or telephones the office, as prearranged. Paging systems are becoming more and more complex and some of them can now store a number of messages and can receive calls from more than one source, with differently toned bleeps to distinguish between callers. They are available from British Telecom and other companies.

**Answering machines**
In very small companies where the offices are likely to remain
unoccupied during the lunch hour or if telephone calls are likely to
come in at any hour of the day and night, a telephone answering
machine is usually installed. When switched on, the answering
machine will ask callers to leave a message. This is recorded on
magnetic tape and can be played back when someone returns to the
office.

The most up-to-date answering machines are electronic and
incorporate a number of advanced facilities, such as displays telling
you how many messages the machine has stored and remote play-
back, which means that you can phone up from outside the office
and have your messages played back to you over the telephone.

**Radio telephones**
Finally, it is possible to phone from a car to most places in the
United Kingdom, Western Europe and even further afield, as well
as to ships and oil platforms in coastal waters. To use the
Radiophone service the car has to be equipped with a receiving and
transmitting set, as well as a suitable aerial.

Radio telephones are proving so popular that the airwaves are
becoming crowded and demand far exceeds supply, but it looks as if
a new solution is already on the horizon – cellular radio. Several
companies are competing to secure a licence to operate this new
system, with the result that, before long, most business executives
will probably sport a radio telephone in their car.

## Making calls

As for the actual technique of handling both outgoing and incoming
calls, the method you adopt will depend partly on the custom
prevalent in your company, and partly on your chief's preference.
These days many executives dial their own calls, but some still like
their secretary to get all calls for them. Some executives want a
secretary to screen incoming calls carefully; others feel they should
take most calls without a preliminary grilling. The two sections
which follow must therefore be adapted to the method preferred by
your own particular company and chief.

In some companies only the telephone operator is permitted to dial outside calls. In others, you pick up the phone, ask for a line and dial the call yourself. If this is the custom where you work, make sure you have a set of relevant telephone directories permanently nearby. Your local telephone directory will give you a list of the various other directories available, together with an order form. You should also have the Yellow Pages, which list business subscribers classified according to the business they are in; the British Telecom booklet listing the dialling codes; and, if you make many calls overseas, the special blue guide to telephoning abroad.

Your card index will be invaluable to you when it comes to making phone calls (see Chapter 11). You will have reason to appreciate any reminder which you write by a phone number. Such pieces of information as 'Visits branches every Friday' or 'Society lunch on Wednesdays' will save you wasting time trying to contact people when they are not available.

You might prefer to keep a list of the telephone numbers you need regularly, complete with area codes, in a personal telephone directory. You can get one free of charge from British Telecom. You may be lucky enough to have a 'memory phone' or 'callmaker'. These are devices which not only store up to four hundred telephone numbers, but can call them up for you at the touch of one, two or three buttons.

If you are telephoning on your own behalf, have all your material ready before making the call. If there are several points to discuss, jot them down first. It is also useful to mention how many items you want to discuss, since some people have a way of hanging up as soon as one point is settled. Another technique which saves time is to give your conversation a title, as it were. If, for instance, you want to raise a point about a session at the forthcoming Sales Conference, you can start off by saying 'About your talk for the Sales Conference', then go on to say your piece. This puts the listener in the picture straightaway, and helps you to deliver the message with far fewer preliminary words. It also enables him to get the relevant file or notes and follow the gist of what you are saying to better advantage.

If you have three entirely different things to say, you might open the conversation in this way: 'Oh, good morning, Mr Brown. Sally Jones of Aldrige's here. Just three small points – first, your talk for the Sales Conference . . .'. You make your point, and when Mr

Brown has had a chance to reply, you announce the subject of your second topic, and then your third. Needless to say, your material should be carefully laid out in front of you, and you should know exactly what you want to say and how best to say it.

When making a call for the chief, if the person is not available, ask the secretary to get him to call back. If you yourself wish to speak to him, ask his secretary when it would be convenient for you to call again.

If you get a wrong number, apologise and hang up. It is rude to hang up without an apology and irritating to give long explanations. When you get a crossed line, replace your receiver and dial again. If you are disconnected in the course of a conversation, replace the receiver and dial the number again.

Although all inland long-distance numbers can now be dialled, it is still possible to get them through the operator, and this is what you should do if you have any difficulty in getting a number. Your *Telephone Dialling Codes* booklet will tell you how to do it.

A great many countries abroad can also be dialled direct. This is known as International Direct Dialling (IDD). Be prepared to wait up to a minute before you are connected, because IDD calls have to travel long distances. You should also bear in mind that tones used in other countries are usually different from those used in the UK. A description of these tones is given in both the general *Telephone Dialling Codes* booklet mentioned above and the special international booklet. In addition there are leaflets for individual countries, available free of charge from British Telecom.

When making calls abroad, you should bear in mind that there is usually a time differential between the United Kingdom and countries overseas. The difference in time can be up to twelve hours, and a map illustrating the differentials is given in the British Telecom booklet. If you have any difficulties getting an international call, contact the International Operator.

Telephone calls are charged at so much per minute, depending on distance and time. In the UK a peak rate operates from 9 a.m. to 1 p.m., a standard rate between 8 a.m. and 9 a.m. and between 1 p.m. and 6 p.m., and a cheap rate after 6 p.m. and at weekends. This means that a higher rate is charged just at the time when most business people are likely to want to use the telephone.

Not many companies can afford to put off all telephoning until the afternoon, but if you have any non-urgent calls to make, it is well worthwhile making them in the afternoon. The only other contribution you can make to keeping down the cost of telephoning is to keep your conversations brief, and to limit personal calls to essentials and emergencies.

## Receiving calls

The routine to follow with incoming calls will also be dictated by your chief's wishes. On no account should you take it upon yourself to screen incoming calls without first asking the chief. A secretary to the managing director of a small company may well take all calls for the company. If such is the case, then announce the name of the company in a cheerful alert tone of voice. 'Brown and Company, good morning', is an excellent way of doing it.

If there is a switchboard operator and you take only your chief's calls, then simply announce yourself, and say 'Mr Smith's secretary'. Pick up your pencil at the same time as the receiver, and be ready to note the name of the caller and the message. If the caller is a well-trained secretary or a thoughtful person who knows the value of time, he or she will say 'Mr Jones calling Mr Smith'. In such cases simply announce the call and put it through.

If Mr Smith is not in, you should say 'I'm afraid Mr Smith is not in his office. May I have him call you back?' Note the name of the caller, the company (if any) and the telephone number on the appropriate telephone message form, if the company supplies them. Add the date and time of the call, and a clear message, such as 'Mr Jones of Jones and Laughlin phoned, and would like you to call back.' If the caller volunteers additional information, add it to the message, but do not 'pump' him. He may prefer to say his piece in his own way.

It is far more polite to suggest your chief returning the call than to ask the caller to try again later, as so many secretaries do. Business is a two-way affair and any businessman worth his salt should meet his callers half-way. The girl who told a caller 'I think he's too important to call you back' had her priorities quite wrong. Good businessmen should never try to convey the idea that they are 'important'; they are simply people with a job of work to do.

If the chief seldom bothers to return calls, then try and remind him to do so. It is bad manners and bad business to ignore people's calls. A tactful reminder is all that is needed. You might say 'Shall I call back Mr Jones of Jones and Laughlin for you?' Take the phone message with you, make the connection, then tear up the message. If necessary you can proceed in this way until all the messages disappear from your chief's desk. Of course, if he curtly replies 'I don't want to speak to the man', the subject should be dropped immediately.

Tact and diplomacy are your greatest assets when it comes to screening telephone calls. If someone calls to whom you are sure the chief does not want to speak, you are acting as a filter when you say 'I'm terribly sorry, Mr Jenkins, but Mr Smith is not in his office at the moment.' When an irate customer rings up and begins to vent his wrath against the company, its product and your chief, you are acting as a buffer if you say 'I'm terribly sorry you've been having so much trouble with. . . . I know Mr Smith will be very distressed to hear about it.' If the caller continues to rage, let him. Hear him out, make further soothing noises, and then pass the call to the chief – if you have been so directed. Probably by this time the customer will have calmed down, and the chief will be able to restore his goodwill and put the matter right.

You should guard your chief's image and cover up for him whenever necessary. *Never* say 'He's not back from lunch yet', or 'He's not in yet'. This gives a bad impression, as it conveys the idea that the chief is indulging in a prolonged lunch and lingering over his brandy, or that he is a reluctant riser and often late for the office. Do not say where the chief is unless it is appropriate, for example if he is away on a lengthy business trip.

One might say that the ideal technique for a secretary to adopt on the telephone is to maintain a welcoming manner to all, yet to keep some people away some of the time without their realising it.

## Other telecommunications services

If you study the green pages in your telephone directory you will see how many other services British Telecom offers. Here are the main ones:

**Personal calls**   If you want to speak to someone who is difficult to contact, you can book a personal call at a small extra charge. It is also possible to book an international personal call, to a person, a specified telephone extension number or department, or to someone who speaks a particular language. This is a very useful service, as getting hold of the right person overseas is not always an easy matter.

**Conference calls**   The audio teleconference system called Orator enables two groups of up to six people to be linked together over two ordinary telephone exchange lines. This service can save considerable travelling time and expense since meetings can be held between offices hundreds of miles apart simply by making a phone call and pressing the appropriate buttons in the control unit. Obviously these conference calls can only be made between two groups equipped with Orator.

**Freefone**   This is a service which enables customers, employees or the general public to telephone an organisation without cost to themselves. The Freefone number can be displayed in advertisements or in the telephone directory. Callers dial the operator, then quote the Freefone number. The cost to Freefone subscribers relates to the size of the area chosen and includes the charge applicable for an operator-connected call, plus a service charge for each call.

**Transferred charge calls**   The cost of a call can be transferred to the called number if the call is accepted when the operator offers it. This service is also available to some countries abroad. It is a service not unfamiliar to students phoning their homes from a call box, but is also useful for sales representatives and other employees phoning their offices from the 'field'.

**Credit card calls**   This service enables you to make calls from any telephone, including a call box, without making immediate payment. Credit card calls are charged to your telephone account. There is a charge for each card and an additional fee for each call. The service can be used for inland and international calls, and also from many countries abroad. This too is a useful service for sales representatives or other company staff who have frequent need to keep in touch with the office.

A variation on this service is the payphone which requires no coins but simply the insertion of a special card entitling the user to so many minutes of conversation. When the call is ended, the card is returned to the user for further use.

**Datel**   Companies employing computer processes can use British Telecom Datel services, which operate over the telephone network, to enable their computer to communicate with distant sites. A Datel service comprises a telephone line connected to a translation device called a *modem*, which allows privately owned data processing equipment to work over the telephone network. The line may be a normal exchange line or a privately-leased circuit, depending on the speed required and the anticipated usage. There is a range of Datel services to meet different requirements as to application, speed and volume of data transmission. Most Datel services can also be used to much of Europe, the USA and a number of other countries.

**PSS**   Also known as SwitchStream One, PSS is an alternative to Datel. It is a public network, like the telephone network, but provided exclusively for carrying data. PSS allows interconnection between terminals working at different speeds and also, via an international service, to other parts of the world. PSS is used for remote order processing, credit verification and on-line retrieval.

**Teletex**   This is a telecommunication service for text communication in which terminals are used to transmit, receive and reproduce typewriter quality texts. With a Teletex terminal, secretaries can prepare a letter with equipment which looks very like a modern typewriter and, by pressing the appropriate buttons, send it directly over telecommunications links to a single addressee, or to several destinations. Teletex can be used over the public telephone network or PSS.

**Questions**
1   Draw up a check-list of information which you would give to a junior making an international telephone call for the first time.    (LCC PSC Office Organisation and Secretarial Procedures)
2   Describe the main features of two of the following, mentioning the type of circumstances in which they are likely to be used:

(*a*)  Callmakers;
(*b*)  Telephone answering systems;
(*c*)  Coin/card-operated telephones.     (LCC PSC Office Organisation and Secretarial Procedures)
3  Explain the following telephone services and suggest circumstances in which they might be used: personal call, Freefone, radiophone.
4  Why is it good business practice for an executive to return a call if he was not available when the caller first tried to contact him? What can a secretary do to encourage this practice?
5  Tact and diplomacy are two of the secretary's most valuable assets on the telephone. What would you tell a caller if:
(*a*)  It was 9.30 and your chief was not yet in the office?
(*b*)  It was 15.00 and your chief had not returned from lunch?
6  Which telephone directories and other information would you be sure to have on your desk if you were responsible for making all company calls?
7  Your company is anxious to reduce the amount it spends on telephone call charges. Suggest a variety of ways in which it might tackle the problem.     (LCC PSC Office Organisation and Secretarial Procedures)

# 8

# Appointments and Visitors

In none of your functions as secretary will you have more need for poise, tact, courtesy and intuition than in receiving the chief's visitors. At times firmness will be needed too, and you will always have to temper all these qualities with the need to keep things moving and to spend the minimum time on social chatter and other niceties. Time is money in business, and it is therefore important to be courteous yet brisk. It *is* a tall order, but by no means impossible.

## The diary

A properly kept diary is a prerequisite to the smooth handling of visitors, although obviously the diary has other purposes, such as keeping a record of expenses. Most secretaries keep a duplicate of the chief's diary on their own desk, and most executives keep a second diary in their pockets. This gives us a total of three diaries for the same set of appointments. There is sometimes even a fourth, when the chief's spouse is an equally busy executive and they have a number of social engagements together. In this situation you will have to be very alert and work closely with both of them if things are to run smoothly every time.

Some secretaries make appointments for the chief without checking with him every time. Obviously you would not do this unless it had been previously agreed. If such is the arrangement, you should record the appointment in the chief's diary as well as your own. You cannot afford to wait until the next time you go into his office.

The more usual procedure is for the secretary to ask on the

intercom 'Is it all right for me to book Mr So-and-So in at such-and-such a time next Wednesday?' Some executives make most of their appointments themselves, without even mentioning them to their secretary. In such cases they should be copied from his diary into your own, and the receptionist alerted when to expect visitors.

Appointments involving the chief's spouse must be checked first with his or her secretary, as well as with your own chief. If the chief makes his own appointments in the evening and enters them in his pocket diary, he may well need to be reminded to transfer them to his desk diary where appropriate. If you have this kind of a chief, always make sure he has not forgotten to make the transfer. It is easy to forget, and the consequences can be embarrassing.

The chief's outside appointments will obviously also go in his desk diary and he will usually make the entries himself. On referring to the day's 'tickler' file in the morning (see Chapter 11), enter into the chief's diary any reminders you find. Some like to be reminded of personal commitments, and then the reminder should be made a few days before the event. On no account, however, should you carry out such a task unless specifically requested to do so.

## Receiving visitors

The actual procedure to follow with callers will depend on the size of the company, how up-to-date and well laid out the building is, and the customs prevailing in the company.

In a large business there is usually a commissionaire or reception-ist in the hall. In such cases, type for them a list of the expected visitors and times of arrival. Some large companies have special forms for the purpose, to be completed and sent to the front desk.

When the visitor arrives, the commissionaire or receptionist will announce him by phone. What happens next again varies from company to company, and you should carry out the procedure laid down, or agree one with your chief. In some cases the secretary goes down to the hall and greets the visitor. In other instances the visitor is asked to go up to the relevant floor where the secretary will meet him. In yet other cases, the visitor is told to go to a stated room, which is usually the secretary's office. Sometimes the com-missionaire takes the visitor all the way to the secretary's office.

You may not work for a large company, however. Then the

chief's visitors may come face to face with a telephone operator peering at them through a tiny window, or there may be a reception-ist only two doors from your own office. Whatever the case, still send along a list of callers so that no one arrives for an appointment without getting a smile of recognition and welcome from whomever he first approaches. If you make an appointment during the day for the same day, inform the receptionist. This technique should entire-ly eliminate that insulting question 'Have you an appointment?' which inexperienced staff sometimes put to a visiting senior execu-tive.

When meeting your visitor, you may need to make sure you have the right person. If the lift stops and disgorges several people you will usually be able to spot your visitor, since he will be looking out for you. You can then smile and ask 'Mr Brown?', and when he confirms your deduction, you can go on to say 'I'm Mary Smith, Mr White's secretary. Would you care to come this way?'

If you have to take him for a long walk down a maze of corridors, or if you have met in the hall to take him up in the lift, you should certainly pass a casual remark such as 'Did you have any trouble finding us?', or something about the weather, or parking his car. You will naturally have alerted the chief as soon as the visitor was announced, so when you reach the office, simply open the door for him and say 'Mr Brown to see you.' In many instances, of course, the visitor will be well known both to your chief and to you, so he will find his own way up to your office, and all you need to do is to greet him and say 'Do go in, Mr White's expecting you!'

**Coping with delays**

It not infrequently happens that, although the chief was expecting Mr Brown, he has been detained by another visitor, or otherwise needs a few minutes' respite. In such cases, ask Mr Brown to sit down and whether he wants to relieve himself of his coat, and make sure there is some suitable reading matter on the table. This should be so, because you will have checked in the morning.

This procedure applies if the chief needs only a few minutes. If a longer delay is involved, then apologise: 'I'm awfully sorry, Mr Brown, but I'm afraid Mr White has been detained. Do you mind waiting for a few minutes?' Once Mr Brown is comfortably settled in a chair, he can be offered a cup of tea or coffee. It is usually welcome and helps a visitor resign himself to being kept waiting, despite having arrived at the appointed time.

If the delay is to be very long, again apológise, explain the reason, and let the visitor decide whether he wants to wait, or prefers to return another day. In the latter eventuality, then he must, of course, be permitted to name the day and hour. Such a situation should, of course, occur only very infrequently, if both the chief and yourself are well organised.

**Terminating visits**
Some executives will go to great lengths to prevent a visitor from overstaying his allotted time, asking their secretaries to give a certain caller half-an-hour and then announce someone else, or come in to remind them about a conference or an outside appointment. Other executives give this kind of treatment only in certain cases. You may agree on a prearranged signal, perhaps a concealed buzzer, which alerts you to appear on the scene and remind him of a vital appointment. Apart from this kind of special arrangement, you should watch the diary while the chief has a visitor, and, if the time of another engagement draws near, you should remind him as discreetly as possible.

**Visitors from within the company**
Visits from the chief's colleagues and subordinates are handled in various ways. Colleagues often just call out 'Is he in?', then charge ahead. If they are good-mannered, and want to discuss a lengthy matter, they usually call on the intercom and ask if it is convenient. If you work for the managing director or company chairman, subordinates may still be encouraged to come along any time they need help either in their work or on a personal matter. This is called the open door policy and it is to be hoped that more and more companies are following it. If you are lucky enough to work for a company which follows this open door policy, you should certainly not try to prevent members of the staff from going to see the chief; quite the contrary. Simply warn them off if he has a visitor, but otherwise reassure them with a smile and say 'It's all right, he is in.'

**Visitors from outside the company**

People from outside the company obviously cannot be allowed to see the chief without an appointment, neither can you cheerfully make an appointment for everyone who wants to see him. This is a delicate situation, but not an impossible one to handle. If you work for a very large company, you will have little trouble with people appearing unexpectedly and demanding an audience with your boss. The smaller the company, however, the greater the chance of such people turning up more and more frequently to interrupt the day.

The first and most important rule to observe is that it is your duty to be courteous and patient with everyone, regardless of whether they have an appointment, and regardless of whether they look 'important'. It is always out of place to adopt a supercilious air, and classifying human beings as important or unimportant is never part of a secretary's duty; neither is the attitude that the chief is a demigod and that talking to certain people would be beneath his dignity. Whether managing director or sales manager, he is simply a company executive doing his best to do a good job – no more and no less. It follows that it is his business to see anyone whose proposition may be of interest to the company, and it is up to him to decide who these people are.

People who turn up without an appointment are usually selling something: a product, a service, or themselves. If they are good salesmen they try to secure an appointment beforehand, but they may not succeed in doing so and it is perfectly legitimate for them to try the personal approach if all else fails. It is not for you, therefore, to treat them like inferior beings. Your own company probably sells a product too. So if a salesman presents himself to see the chief, take his card and ask him to explain a little more about his proposition so that you can find out if the chief will see him.

It may become apparent that he should be talking to the purchasing officer, in which case say so and suggest that he make a prior appointment. Cooperate with him to the extent of giving him the name of the purchasing officer. You could suggest he telephones to make an appointment, or you might even phone the purchasing officer's secretary and ask whether he could see the salesman right away. The answer might well be 'No', but you will have tried to be helpful.

If the chief *is* the purchasing officer, then of course you should ask on the intercom if he will see Mr So-and-So, a representative for Such-and-Such a company. If the answer is 'No', then inform the caller pleasantly and regretfully.

A salesman representing an office supplies or office equipment company may know he has little chance of seeing the chief, but will welcome an opportunity of showing you the latest in carbon paper, stationery or filing equipment. By all means let him show you samples, and keep his card. It is extremely useful to know what is new on the market in these lines, and when ordering new supplies your chief will probably be glad to follow your recommendations.

The caller may be an artist anxious to show off his portfolio, a designer of some sort, or other creative person hoping to get a 'break'. Deal kindly with all of them and try to help them if you can – there may well be a genius among them!

**Dealing with journalists**
The caller may be a journalist anxious to get an 'angle' for his story, although even journalists usually phone for an appointment first. Don't imagine that it is a waste of the chief's time to speak to the press: nothing could be further from the truth. It is in his and the company's best interest not only to receive the journalist, but to do so courteously and to answer his questions as openly and with as much honesty as he can muster. Announce the journalist, there-fore, and try to give as clear an indication of the object of his visit as possible. Say, for instance: 'Mr Mitchell of the *Express and Star* is here and he is wondering whether he could have a word with you about the closedown of the Hackney plant. Shall I send him in?'

If the chief is out, or prefers not to see the reporter, never take it upon yourself to answer his questions, however obliquely put. You are very sorry but you simply don't know anything about the impending closure of the Hackney plant. No, you don't know whether there has been any labour trouble. No, you haven't heard the men say anything. You never go near Hackney, in fact. No, you've no idea whether orders have been falling off. You're terribly sorry, in fact, but you simply cannot throw any light on the matter at all. However you should remain polite and courteous, and if he wants to know the name of the works manager, you should tell him, *and* give him the phone number of the Hackney works if he should ask for it. Of course, if your company employs a press officer, you should have referred the reporter to him in the first place.

**Personal callers**

Other people who may occasionally call to see the chief without appointment are friends or business associates, relatives and his spouse. The sooner you get to know who these are the better. You will soon know whether the chief expects them to go right in to his office, or whether they should be announced and treated like everyone else. Sometimes you can even ask. The chief may say 'Oh, by the way, my wife will be in some time this afternoon.' Then you can ask 'Shall I show her right in?'

It can be rather difficult if someone suddenly appears and asks to 'Say hallo to Mr Brown'. The important thing is not to eye him with suspicion, as so many secretaries do, as if perfectly convinced he must be an interloper. Simply get his name and transmit his message exactly, either by putting your head into the chief's office or by the intercom: 'Mr Hastings is here wondering whether he can come in and say "hallo" to you.' Callers are annoyed if you do not transmit the right message, and from your chief's point of view it is easier for him to assess the situation if you relay exactly what the caller said.

# Phone calls during conferences

Well organised executives ask their secretaries not to interrupt them with telephone calls if they have a meeting or a visitor in their office. Simply take messages and pass them on as soon as the meeting is concluded.

At times, however, something urgent crops up, and the chief must be alerted right away. In such cases, type out the message clearly, go unobtrusively into the chief's office and hand it discreetly to him. He can then scribble a reply, or apologise to those present and pick up the telephone. Follow the same procedure if the meeting is in another office to which you have access.

A phone call for a visitor with the chief should be put through in the ordinary way. If a meeting is in progress, however, you would be better advised to follow the same procedure as previously outlined. Write the message on a slip of paper and hand it discreetly to the visitor. If he says 'I'll phone them back later', take down the name

and phone number of the caller, and offer the visitor the use of the
phone when he emerges from the meeting.

**Questions**
1  How would you deal with a visitor who arrives without an
   appointment?
2  You have made an appointment for your employer but need to
   confirm this with him. How have you indicated the appointment
   in your diary?        (Pitman Secretarial Practice Intermediate)
3  The switchboard operator has passed to you a message taken
   from the telephone answering machine in which a local newspaper reporter has stated that he wishes to interview Mr Watson
   (your chief), whom he knows personally, about the rumoured
   redundancies and that he will be calling at your offices this
   morning. You know that Mr Watson does not want information
   released to the press, nor interviews with reporters on this
   subject until further and final company decisions have been
   made. State what steps you will take and why in dealing with this
   matter.        (RSA Secretarial Duties Stage II)
4  Waiting in the reception hall is an executive who has an appointment to see your chief at 14.30 hours. The latter, however, has
   been unavoidably detained outside the office and he has just
   phoned to tell you that he will not arrive until 15.00 hours. It is
   now 14.35 hours. How will you handle the visitor?
5  Your chief is closeted in his office with an important buyer from
   abroad. He has asked you to hold all telephone calls. However,
   your chief's superior wishes to speak to him urgently, and so you
   must get in touch with him at once. How do you handle the
   situation?

# 9

# Meetings: Formal and Informal

The objects of a business meeting are to impart information, to discuss problems, to plan strategies, to allocate tasks and to reach decisions. There are sales meetings, committee meetings, staff meetings, planning and board meetings, and the Annual General Meeting, usually known as the AGM. Apart from the latter, most of these meetings are of the informal kind, and it will frequently be your arduous task to reach everyone by telephone or memorandum to make sure they can be present. Even if you work for the managing director or the company chairman your task will not be easy, and you will need a great deal of patience and persistence to get everyone to agree to a day and time.

Even if the meeting is to be an informal one, you will frequently be given an agenda to type and send to all participants, if your chief is calling the meeting. If he is being summoned to one, on the other hand, he will give you notes on points he is to make and perhaps the facts and figures to support his arguments. While the meeting is in progress your task will be either to take telephone messages and keep everyone temporarily at bay, or else to attend the meeting and take notes.

## Formal meetings

Formal meetings are quite a different matter and, if you do not understand what they entail and just what goes on, you may find them rather forbidding. However, take heart, as many company executives find them equally forbidding at first. A formal meeting is one which is conducted along lines similar to, but not identical with, parliamentary procedure. Various kinds of meeting are conducted formally. The two most important ones for a business concern are the Annual General Meeting, at which the company reports to the shareholders on its stewardship during the previous year, and the board meeting, at which major policy decisions are made. Then there are formal or semi-formal general and committee meetings, either connected with the business or with outside interests such as professional societies, trade or other associations, political or labour organisations, church or school work, and so on.

Your chief's role will almost certainly vary from meeting to meeting. He may be chairman at one meeting – that is, he will conduct the meeting; he may be treasurer – that is, hold the purse strings – for another organisation and will report on his stewardship at that meeting; he may be secretary at a third meeting, and an ordinary committee member on other occasions. You yourself may well be elected secretary to a committee connected, say, with social activities, but of course no one can elect you without your consent! As you will see, the secretary is the one who does all the administrative work of the committee: sending out notices, preparing the agenda, taking notes, writing the minutes, and so on.

## Notice of meeting

Twenty-one days' notice in writing must be given for an Annual General Meeting and fourteen days is usual for other formal meetings. The notice must specify the date, time and place of the meeting and should normally state the business to be discussed. The notice must be sent to all those who have a right to attend, that is to all members of the association in the case of an Annual General Meeting, and to all members of the committee in the case of a committee meeting. Responsibility for preparing and sending out the notice of meeting rests with the secretary – by which we mean the elected secretary in this case.

## Agenda

The agenda is also prepared by the secretary, in agreement with the chairman. It is the programme of the business to be transacted at the meeting, in the order in which the items will be taken. It must also

THE BRITSHIRE CONSERVATION ASSOCIATION

The Annual General Meeting of the Britshire Conservation Association will be held at the Association Head Office, Regent House, Beech Road, Maidenhead on Thursday, 3 March 19-- at 2000 hours.

A G E N D A

1  Minutes of last meeting

2  Matters arising

3  Correspondence and apologies for absence

4  Chairman's annual report

5  Secretary's annual report

6  Treasurer's annual report, statement of accounts
   and balance sheet

7  Election of officers

8  Conservation programme for school children

9  Any other business

**Fig. 9.1**   An agenda for an AGM

include the date, time and place of the meeting. The agenda for an
Annual General Meeting is shown in Fig. 9.1.

Sometimes the apologies for absence are read first and the
minutes of the previous meeting follow. If, however, a chairman has
to be elected, then this becomes the first business of the meeting, a
temporary chairman being selected to organise the election of a
permanent chairman.

It is a good idea to type the agenda with an extra wide right-hand margin to be used for notes. The chairman and secretary usually have this done on their own copy, but everyone appreciates it. In addition to the extra wide margin, the chairman's copy of the agenda contains further relevant details to help him run the meeting. For instance, he will have the names of those who sent in apologies and the letters to be read. He will have the names of the nominees for office and possibly a file containing other information, perhaps on conservation programmes for schoolchildren run by other conservation associations in this example.

If it is an Annual General Meeting, as in Fig. 9.1, then a copy of the agenda should be sent to all members of the organisation. If it is a committee meeting, then it should go to committee members only. If the agenda has been prepared sufficiently far in advance it can go out at the same time as the notice of meeting, or can actually be incorporated in it. Otherwise it is sufficient to send it out in good time for everyone to become familiar with the contents and make their own preparations.

A sufficient number of copies of the agenda should be made so that one may be placed before each seat at the meeting. In addition, the agenda of each meeting is inserted in the agenda book, which is presented to the chairman. This copy becomes *the* agenda. It is usually inserted on a left-hand page, the opposite page being left blank for notes.

## Preliminary formalities

It is customary for the chairman to take the head of the table, with the secretary on the right and the treasurer on the left. The other committee members are free to sit anywhere at the table. At a large meeting the committee is usually accommodated on a platform and the rest of the members are seated in the main hall.

It is the secretary's responsibility to see that every member has a copy of the agenda, and to record the names of those present. There are various ways of doing the latter. An attendance register can be placed at the entrance to the hall for members to sign as they enter, or a sheet of paper can be passed around for signature once everyone is seated. This method greatly facilitates the secretary's task of identifying the speakers for the purpose of taking notes for the minutes.

The Companies Act 1948 stipulates that a meeting can only carry out its business if a minimum number of those eligible to attend, called a *quorum*, is present. The Act specifies that, in the case of a private company, two members constitute a quorum, while three are required for any other company. However, the minimum number is usually specified in an organisation's Articles of Association. Before opening the meeting, it is the chairman's duty to make sure that a quorum is present. The business then proceeds in the order laid down in the agenda.

## Procedure

Once preliminary formalities are over, the actual business of the meeting begins with the consideration of the proposals, called *motions*, put before it. A motion is usually stated in writing before the meeting, as in the specimen agenda on p. 116, with the name of the person suggesting it (the *proposer*) and the person supporting it (the *seconder*). Once a motion has been proposed and seconded, it is open to debate and anyone can rise and speak on it, always addressing himself to the chair, that is, prefacing his remarks with the words 'Mr Chairman' or 'Madam Chairman', as the case may be.

No one may speak more than once on the same question, except the proposer of the motion, who is entitled to reply to criticism or to give explanations or amplifications. This is known as the *right of reply*. Inevitably, there will be dissenting voices. Quite apart from those who are entirely against the motion, there may be those who think it is too extreme and those who feel it does not go far enough. Others will feel that it could be worded more clearly, or more forcefully, or more in accord with their own thinking on the subject. These dissenters will therefore want to suggest alterations to the motion, which are called *amendments*. Amendments too have their proper form. They should either leave out words, insert words or substitute a different form of words. Amendments may be proposed by anyone except the proposer and seconder of the original motion. Amendments do not need a seconder by law, but it is the almost universal custom to require a seconder, and indeed the rules, standing orders or other regulations of many bodies require it.

The seconder of an amendment may either make his speech in favour when he rises to second the amendment, or later on, but he may not make any further remark during the discussion which follows. In the 'popular procedure' it is the general practice to vote on the amendment before voting on the motion which it seeks to amend. If the amendment is carried, it is incorporated into the original motion, which is then known as the *substantive motion*. Each amendment is treated in the same fashion until the subject is exhausted. Finally, the motion as a whole is put to the vote.

Committees often vote by a show of hands. The chairman will say 'Those in favour of the motion', and all those in favour will raise their hands. After a quick tally, the chairman will say 'Those against' and the 'noes' will raise *their* hands.

More accurate measures are needed in some cases. At a share-holders' meeting, for instance, the holder of ten shares of company stock must be differentiated from the holder of ten thousand shares. So each member present will register his vote on a card and the weight of his vote will be assessed according to the colour of the card. Absent shareholders can vote by proxy, using the voting card which will have been sent to them with the notice of meeting.

If the identity of voters is not needed or desired, a *ballot* can be taken. Voting slips are put into a ballot box and *tellers* are appointed to count the votes.

A motion may be passed *unanimously*, that is all members vote in favour of it, or it may be passed *nem. con.* (*nemine contradicente*) or *nem. dis.* (*nemine dissentiente*), that is, no one opposed it though some members *abstained*, i.e. refrained from voting. Sometimes the chairman has what is known as a *casting vote*, an extra vote to enable him to tip the scales in one direction or the other if the voting is equal.

When the main business of the meeting is concluded, miscel-laneous matters can be raised under *Any other Business*; the date of the next meeting is either set or confirmed, where pertinent, and the meeting is closed. If it has not been possible to conclude all the business on the agenda, the committee can agree to *adjourn* and meet again on an agreed date.

**Some useful terms**

Here are a few other terms you may hear in connection with formal meetings:

*Standing orders* are the rules laid down by an organisation regulating the manner in which its business is to be conducted.

*Ad hoc*   Something done for a specific purpose. Accordingly, an 'ad hoc committee' is one set up to study a specific question or to carry out a particular piece of work. Such committees are sometimes called special purpose committees.

*Co-option* is the power given to a committee to allow others to serve on it. People brought into the meeting in this way are known as *co-opted members*.

*Ex-officio* literally means 'Arising out of his office'. Accordingly, an ex officio member of a committee holds the place by virtue of his office.

*Status quo*   This means the state of affairs that exists at a particular time, so 'to maintain the status quo' means there is to be no change.

*Sub-committees* may be appointed by a committee to carry out a specific part of the work. The sub-committee must report periodically to the committee which has delegated the work to it.

## The minutes

During the meeting, the committee secretary should pay close attention and make a note of decisions taken. These notes will serve in good stead when it comes to write up the minutes. If they are to give an accurate reflection of events, the minutes of a meeting should be written very carefully. Meetings of clubs and societies are often casually written and include only the decisions made. The minutes of directors' meetings, however, must conform to the Companies Act 1948 and should therefore include the appointment of officers made by the directors, the names of the directors present, and all the resolutions and proceedings.

It is a good plan to adopt a pattern for the minutes, as this makes them much easier both to write and to read. The following is a reasonable plan:

1   Place, date, and time the meeting began;
2   The name of the chairman;

3   The name of the other officials present, as well as all others present in the case of a small gathering, or the number of members present in the case of larger bodies;

4   Reference to the formalities gone through before the actual business of the meeting, i.e. reading of the notice of meeting, the minutes of the previous meeting, and so on;

5   An outline of the business discussed and decisions made;

6   Details of any other business discussed, if any;

7   Date fixed for the next meeting, if applicable;

8   Time when the meeting closed.

All these details must be recorded as concisely as possible, but the exact wording of every motion passed must be given, as well as the name of each proposer and seconder.

The minutes should be written in a bound *Minute Book*, which is the official legal record of a committee's proceedings. In the interest of speed, however, they are often typed on loose leaves. If this is done, each sheet should be initialled by the chairman, and the book should be locked away, to guard against tampering and page substitutions.

Draft minutes are often circulated and corrected before the next meeting. In such cases the chairman suggests that the minutes be taken 'as read', to which everyone usually agrees only too readily. The chairman then signs them, and no further alterations to them are permitted.

As we said earlier in this chapter, you may well be elected secretary to the social club committee at your company, and if such were the case, the minutes you would produce after a committee meeting might look like Fig. 9.2.

Finally, if it is your chief who is holding a meeting, you will want to make sure there are enough chairs around the table, that a pitcher of water and glass are at hand by the chairman's seat, that paper for note-taking is before each seat and that coffee or tea is served at the appropriate time, either by yourself or whoever is in charge of refreshments.

## Social functions

There is hardly a company which does not hold some kind of work-related social function during the course of the year. There

THE HAPPY COMPANY PLC

SOCIAL CLUB COMMITTEE

Minutes of the meeting held in the
canteen of the Company's Registered
Office at 25 Greene Street, London,
EC2 5QX, on Wednesday, 23 March 19--

Present

Mrs M Johnson (in the chair)
Miss D Merryweather
Mr Q Soams
Mr A Tappy
Miss V Best (Secretary)

| | | |
|---|---|---|
| 1 | MINUTES | The minutes of the last meeting were read, adopted and signed by the chairman. |
| 2 | MATTERS ARISING | There were no matters arising out of the minutes. |
| 3 | APOLOGIES | Apologies were received from Miss J Read, due to pressure of work. |
| 4 | SUMMER OUTING | Miss Merryweather and Mr Soams had investigated the possibilities of a river trip and their final suggestions centred around (a) hiring a longboat for a round trip from Windsor, or (b) hiring the Sheriff's Barge at Maidenhead. After a lengthy discussion on the merits of the two trips, it was |
| | | RESOLVED that the Company Chairman be asked to approach the Sheriff's Office with a view to hiring the Barge. |
| | | The final details would be discussed at the next meeting. |
| 5 | ANY OTHER BUSINESS | Mr Tappy requested details of the presentation arrangements for Mr Galbraith's retirement in June. As the Chairman had an appointment to speak to the management on this matter in the near future, it was decided to leave this item until the next meeting. |
| 6 | DATE OF NEXT MEETING | This was arranged for Wednesday, 17 April, 19-- at 1000 hours. |

Chairman

**Fig. 9.2**  The minutes of a committee meeting

might be an annual dinner-dance, a river trip, a coach outing, or a visit to the theatre; there may be presentations to retiring employees, celebrations for employees who have received public recognition or open days if the company has received an award, 'house-warming' parties, and various events to entertain visitors from abroad.

You would certainly not be expected to organise a large event single-handed, but a small party in your chief's office should be well within your capabilities. How you proceed will rather depend on whether your company has its own catering facilities or whether you have to go to outside caterers. In any event you would be well advised to:

1   Keep abreast with what is going on in the town where you work, and cut out and keep items you find in the newspapers and elsewhere on new restaurants and places of entertainment, special deals for parties, etc.
2   Acquaint yourself with one or two outside caterers, so you are eventually able to compare prices and judge facilities.
3   Include a section for restaurants and night clubs in your card index and fill in details about them as you go along. This is a slow process, as you should not include a restaurant just because it happens to be near the office. Try and get the chief to cooperate in this assessment, and when you know he has taken a client to a certain restaurant, ask him what it was like and include relevant comments on your card.
4   If possible, include at least one guide in your office library, for example the *Good Food Guide* or the *Guide Michelin*.

If an elaborate annual event is involved, such as a dinner-dance or garden party, formal invitations will go out in the chairman's or the managing director's name in the usual way. Otherwise the managing director may send out a circular letter to every member of staff inviting them to the event and asking them to RSVP to you.

You should, of course, have spoken to the company chef or outside caterer well before the invitations go out, and will have taken their advice on menus for fork luncheons, snacks to accompany drinks, and so on. Once you know the exact number of guests expected, you will confirm the arrangements with the caterers, always working in liaison with your chief, who will in any event probably have a clear idea of his requirements.

If it is a question of a small staff party in your chief's office or in the board room, you will need to liaise with whoever is providing the refreshments and check that there is sufficient seating, that cigarettes are available, and that a flower arrangement is provided, if required. When the guests arrive, you will play your part in ushering them in, passing refreshments around and bringing everyone into the picture, paying particular attention to the junior members of staff, who are sometimes over-awed on such occasions.

If the party is for company clients, then you will help in the preliminaries as required, but you should keep out of the way afterwards unless specifically invited by your chief, in which case you should always behave discreetly.

## Questions

1 A new member of staff is to take over from you the task of attending meetings in order to minute the proceedings. In order to help her to do this efficiently, draft some notes on the responsibilities of: (*a*) the chairman; (*b*) the committee secretary.

Explain also what is meant by the following terms: (i) in attendance; (ii) ex officio members; (iii) co-opted members. (LCC PSC Office Organisation and Secretarial Procedures)

2 Because you will be tied up with the arrangements for Mr Watson's trip to the United States, the Works Manager's new secretary, Janet Curtis, will be taking the minutes for the first time at the February Departmental Meeting. She has asked you to explain the meaning of certain terms she has seen in previous minutes, namely:

| | |
|---|---|
| Quorum | Amendment |
| Resolution | Motion |
| Nem. con. | Ex Officio |

(RSA Secretarial Duties Stage II)

3 Give three standard items you would expect to find in an Agenda.   (Pitman Secretarial Practice Intermediate)

4 List and comment briefly on the procedures involved in convening one of a series of committee meetings, i.e. from the conclusion of one meeting up to the point at which the members

attending the next are ready to discuss new business.     (LCC PSC Office Organisation and Secretarial Procedures)

5  You have seen an advertisement for a post as a committee secretary.

   (*a*)  What duties do you think you would have to perform if appointed?

   (*b*)  What questions might you ask about these duties at an interview?     (LCC PSC Office Organisation and Secretarial Procedures)

6  A staff member of long standing is retiring and your chief is presenting him with a parting gift from the company. The presentation is to take place in the Board Room and will be followed by refreshments. The company has canteen staff and refreshments are to be planned without outside help. In what way would you expect to help in organising the party? How will you help your chief to receive the guests and make them welcome?

7  Part of your duties as a secretary involves organising committee meetings.

   (*a*)  Describe how you would prepare the minute book for meetings, and how you would look after it and maintain it as a source of reference when required.

   (*b*)  Some newly-elected members are to attend the next meeting, including two or three from other organisations. What special arrangements would you make before their first meeting?     (LCC PSC Office Organisation and Secretarial Procedures)

# 10

# Travel and Hotel Arrangements

Business executives are travelling more and more these days and it is not impossible for them to have breakfast, lunch and dinner each in a different continent, let alone in a different country. As a result, almost every company, however small, has an account with a travel agency to make all necessary arrangements. In such cases your task will simply consist of phoning the agency and instructing them to make the necessary bookings and hotel reservations.

There are many other matters connected with your employer's business trips which will need your attention, however. Even if a travel agent takes care of the details for you, you must make it your business to know what foreign travel involves, what the various possibilities are, how to make bookings, and, above all, where to go for advice. You will need to keep an eye on the travel agent in case he forgets some important detail, and to remind your chief of the numerous formalities which have to be attended to.

But the occasion will inevitably arise when the agency is simply not trying hard enough, and you will have to pick up the phone and attempt to secure a booking which you have been assured is quite unobtainable.

## Preliminary arrangements

The prime requisite for leaving the country is a valid passport. Passport applications are made on an official form obtainable from your regional passport office. The address can be found in the telephone directory. The completed form, together with two passport photographs, a birth or naturalisation certificate, and the appropriate fee are then taken or posted to the passport office, which issues the passport.

British passports are valid for ten years. Find out when your chief's passport expires, so you can remind him to get a new one. The passport offices are usually busy and it is therefore wise to deal with these formalities well in advance of need, although there is a twenty-four hour emergency service.

Visitor's passports are available at main post offices. They can be used for holidays or unpaid business trips of up to three months, but there are restrictions on the countries which accept them. The conditions are listed on the application form, and should be checked before assuming a full British passport is not required.

British passport holders do not normally need a visa to travel to most Western European countries, but one is required for many countries further afield. Your travel agent will know whether a visa is required, but your safest bet is to ask the consulate of the country in question. They will tell you whether a visa is required, what documents you should present in order to obtain one and, finally, they will issue the visa, which is stamped on the passport. Passport photographs are almost always included in the documents needed, so the hardened traveller always keeps a good supply at hand.

Some countries also require certificates of vaccination and inoculations, and it is far better to take care of such requirements in advance than to get held up at the airport for want of a vaccination. Bear in mind that some inoculations involve two or more injections with several days' interval between them, so do remind your chief to have them done in plenty of time. Information on inoculation requirements can be obtained from the official representative of the country in question, and from travel agents and the travel and tourist offices which many countries maintain in Britain.

Finally, your chief will probably want to take out a travel insurance policy to cover medical expenses, loss of baggage, personal accident, and so on. If he is taking his car abroad, he will want to ensure that his motor insurance is extended to cover the countries he will visit, and that he obtains an International Motor Insurance Certificate, usually called a *green card*.

## Financial arrangements

A traveller abroad will need to take with him a little sterling, which he will find useful for taxis, tips, newspapers, and so on, both on departure and when he gets back, as well as some of the local currency of the countries he is visiting. This will obviate the need to change a traveller's cheque immediately on arrival, which may not always be possible. Foreign currency can be bought at any high street bank, as well as from *Bureaux de Change*, found at stations, airports, and in some city centres. It is advisable to give your bank notice, however, especially if you are buying a less common currency.

Do bear in mind, however, that some foreign countries place restrictions on the amount of their currency that can be taken into and out of their country. Your bank will be able to advise you about this.

Here are some of the other ways a traveller can obtain cash or credit while abroad:

*Travellers' cheques*   These can be bought at high street banks, in sterling, dollars or other currencies. Each cheque is signed by the traveller at the time of purchase. By countersigning a cheque and producing his passport the traveller abroad can cash his cheque on the spot. Many hotels and shops abroad also accept traveller's cheques in payment. Any unused cheques can be sold back to the bank when the traveller returns.

*Credit cards*   These used to be accepted abroad on the same basis as in the UK and could also be used to obtain cash. From 1983 it became necessary to apply for a Eurocheque Card in some cases.

*Open credits*   Whether travelling at home or abroad, you can ask your local bank to arrange an 'open credit' either with a specified branch in the UK or with any overseas bank. You will then be able to obtain cash from the specified bank up to a pre-arranged limit, just as if you were dealing with your local bank.

## Road travel

A substantial proportion of shorter business trips is made by car. In such instances there will be little to concern you, apart from making hotel reservations, since most people take care of their own car travel arrangements.

Certain formalities have to be completed when taking a car abroad, but both the AA and the RAC handle these details for their members and your chief will probably belong to one of these organisations.

## Rail travel

The improved and greatly speeded up domestic rail service has resulted in more people, including businessmen, travelling by train. Businessmen are finding that long drives are very tiring and time-consuming, and that the delay in reaching and leaving airports detracts from the advantages of domestic air travel. Sometimes, therefore, they prefer to travel by train.

If your chief uses the rail services frequently, you will need to be prepared to help him organise his journey by having the timetables handy. The *ABC Rail Guide* covers rail services for the whole of Great Britain and the main international connections. It also gives information on shipping services within the British Isles and to the continent, Hovercraft services, and Motorail services for travellers taking their cars with them. It also gives fares, distances from London, populations, and bus connections.

Read the preliminary pages carefully. They are a mine of information, covering the various services available, tickets and seat reservations, baggage allowances, insurance, rail/road links with airports, British Transport Hotels, and just about everything you need to know about rail travel.

*Cook's Continental Timetable* is a useful guide for those travelling by rail in Europe, and for places even further afield there is the *ABC Air/Rail Europe and Middle East Guide*. In addition you will want to have by you an up-to-date timetable of any particular service which your chief uses regularly.

Rail travel can be first or second class all over Europe. Long distance trains carry sleeper coaches, and berths should be booked in advance. Between London and Manchester there is a Pullman train, which is very luxurious and, of course, slightly more expensive. Some trains have a restaurant car, others a buffet, and sometimes a breakfast tray service is available. An order for this service should be given to the attendant when boarding the train. The *ABC Rail Guide* will give you an indication of the refreshment service available on the various trains.

For long journeys, rail tickets are best booked in advance to save time and delay before departure and it is a good plan also to reserve a seat. Indeed on some Inter-city trains, the Night-Riders and the Pullman, the number of passengers carried is limited to the seating capacity of the train, so it is essential to book in advance. Do this at the railway station booking office or at an appointed travel agency.

## Air travel

The air travel 'bible' is the *ABC World Airways Guide*, published monthly. It includes timetables for all airlines as well as fares and baggage information.

You can make air reservations either through a travel agent or directly through the airline. All travel agents, and some airlines, can arrange for car hire facilities, so that a car is on hand when the traveller arrives. Otherwise the traveller can use the bus provided by the airlines to take him to the city centre. A third alternative is the Railair Link service provided by British Rail to and from many airports.

## Sea voyages

Businessmen seldom travel by sea because of the time involved. This does not mean, however, that you will never have to help your chief to plan a sea voyage or to make the necessary bookings. If this should happen, you should consult the *ABC Shipping Guide*. It is a monthly publication devoted entirely to passenger shipping services, and also gives details of the world's cruises and fly-cruises.

Accommodation can be booked through a travel agent or directly with the shipping company. If you want to investigate the possibility of travelling by passenger-carrying cargo ship, apply direct to the shipping line, as travel agents do not always book these passages. A study of the travel pages in the daily press should prove fruitful.

# Hotel accommodation

Frequently your chief will have a favourite hotel, and will simply ask you to make a booking there. Alternatively, a hotel may have been recommended to him which he wishes to try. Otherwise, if he is travelling within the UK, he will probably consult his AA or RAC book and ask you to try one of the hotels recommended. Here are some of the other sources of information:

*The Financial Times World Hotel Directory* This is especially geared to the businessman, and lists hotels in the main commercial centres of a hundred and fifty countries. It gives numbers and types of room available, conference facilities, audio-visual aids, translation and secretarial services, as well as general information on the countries concerned.

*Hotels and Restaurants* This is the official guide of the British Tourist Authority, and the hotels it recommends have been selected on the basis of suitability for visitors to Britain.

The *ABC Hotel Guide* gives essential information on specially selected hotels throughout the world.

The *ABC Rail Guide* also lists recommended hotels throughout Britain, including special facilities for businessmen. The *British Rail Timetables* give the addresses of British Transport Hotels, which are usually conveniently situated close to stations. This hotel group has a central booking office from which you can book accommodation in any one of its hotels. Several other hotel groups offer this service.

You can also reserve hotel accommodation by using one of the agencies set up for this purpose, which are listed in the yellow pages of the telephone directory. Most of these agencies charge a fee for the service, but others offer a free booking service, since they are set up by the hotels themselves.

Airlines also undertake to make hotel reservations and, of course, you can approach the hotels direct, either by phone, Telex or letter. Alternatively, you can let your travel agent take care of your hotel reservations, as well as seeking his advice on which hotels to use. Do bear in mind, however, that travel agents work only with a given group of hotels and these are naturally the ones they recommend.

If you are handling your own hotel reservation, it is best to do it by letter. If you book by phone or Telex, then confirm by letter. Be exact with regard to date of arrival and length of stay. Say, for instance, 'from the night of 2 January to the night of 5 January, inclusive'. It is always both thoughtful and useful to mention the approximate hour of expected arrival. Hotel rooms should be ready to receive a visitor by noon on the date of arrival. In practice, however, many visitors arrive much later than noon, while people vacating a room may wish to leave a little later. It is therefore good practice to specify the approximate time of arrival to help the hotel organise a smooth changeover. You would therefore be well advised to write, for example: 'Mr Black will be travelling on the 16.30 train from Manchester, due at Blessington at 21.05, and hopes to be in time for dinner'. This will enable the hotel to alert the head waiter, so that Mr Black will be able to have a meal when he arrives.

If, on the other hand, Mr Black is arriving late at night, the hotel should be told, so that they will know he is not missing, or lost, but still on his way from Tokyo or Timbuctoo. They will alert the night porter, and all will be well.

## Preparation and planning

All trips, but especially long ones embracing several countries, should be planned well in advance and a carefully worked out itinerary should be typed out, and kept to as closely as possible. Since most business trips are made on a tight schedule, there are several important points to be borne in mind in the planning if time is not to be wasted.

It would be most undesirable, for instance, to arrive in a country hoping to do business on what turns out to be a public holiday. Moslem holidays, for instance, are movable and fall about eleven days earlier each year. Approximate dates are usually known in advance, but the exact dates will depend on the observation of the moon. Then, of course, you have to bear in mind the religious holidays in Catholic countries, and national holidays such as 14 July in France and Lincoln's Birthday in the USA.

Annual closings should also be considered. Almost all companies on the Continent close down completely for two, three or even four weeks a year, usually in August. It is not inconceivable to arrive in France in time to find the companies one wishes to visit are closed, and then to proceed to Germany and find the same thing. So help your chief on this point by avoiding business trips in August altogether, if possible.

If a *very* short stay in a particular town is envisaged, then it is vital to consider time differences (see page 100) and the local hours of business. Many continental companies observe the long lunch period, usually from 12.00 to 14.00 hours, or even from 12.00 to 15.00 hours, and then continue working until about 19.00 hours. In addition, many countries work different hours in summer and winter, which must also be borne in mind.

To help you get all these details right, the British Overseas Trade Board issues a series of booklets called *Hints to Exporters*. Each booklet covers a different country, and apart from the facts mentioned above, it gives other useful information such as methods of doing business, exchange control regulations, social customs, and even names of hotels and restaurants. You can also obtain the details you need from the local representative of the country concerned, whether consulate, commissioner, or trade institute.

Once the itinerary is settled, the passages booked, and the hotel reservations made, you should type it up in one of the two forms shown in Fig. 10.1 and in the same style for the remainder of the trip. Notice that while flights are fixed, the short journey on 8 November is left open so that a train or car can be taken at whatever time proves convenient.

Your chief will have the top copy of the itinerary, you will retain another, and others should be distributed to all the interested people within the company. You will then need to gather together all papers, correspondence and other material wanted on the journey and put them in a folder in order of use – that is, in our example, first the papers needed in Micropolis, then those needed in Midasville, and so on.

While planning is underway, you should take the precaution of making extra carbons of all correspondence concerning the impending trip, so that you can keep one in the newly created file '198– Trip to France, Germany and Italy', and give the other to the chief for his journey. His copy might be in a distinctive colour to facilitate identification. These arrangements will enable you to keep abreast of what is going on while the chief is away, and, if he telephones from Micropolis, you will know exactly what he is dealing with at that time. All that will remain for you to do then is to make sure he

```
Sun.Nov.3        Lv London airport
                 (Heathrow) at 23.45
                 on Airfrance flight
                 No. 502 for Micro-
                 polis (arr. 01.00)   HOTEL METROPOLE

Mon.Nov.4    )
   to        ) IN MICROPOLIS
Tue.Nov.5    )

Wed.Nov.6        Lv Micropolis at
                 07.00 on Airfrance
                 flight No. 641 for
                 Midasville (arr.
                 08.35 International
                 Airport)             HOTEL EXCELSIOR

Thu.Nov.7        IN MIDASVILLE

Fri.Nov.8        Lv Midasville for
                 Grandeville (a.m.)
                 either by train or
                 car (half hour run) HOTEL RITZ
```

**Fig. 10.1a & b**   Alternative layouts for an itinerary

| | | | |
|---|---|---|---|
| 3 November | 2345 hours | Depart | London airport (Heathrow) Airfrance flight No 502 for Micropolis |
| 4 November | 0100 hours | Arrive | Hotel Metropole |
| 4 November-5 November | | | In Micropolis |
| 6 November | 0700 hours | Depart | Micropolis airport Airfrance flight No 641 for Midasville |
| | 0835 hours | Arrive | International Airport Midasville |
| 7 November | | | In Midasville Hotel Excelsior |

has everything he needs in his briefcase, including dictating equipment and spare cassettes.

## Holding the fort

It would be pleasant to think that while the chief is away you will be able to relax and enjoy a breathing space. Unfortunately, however, you may well find that things do not work out that way. For one thing, you will probably have been especially busy before the departure, so you will now be grateful for the opportunity to catch up with the inevitable backlog of routine work.

Then, of course, work goes on during your chief's absence: letters continue to come in, people continue to phone, salesmen continue to call, and you will need to keep things running smoothly. The chief will have told you how to deal with any special matters which may arise, and you must proceed accordingly. If he has a deputy, then he will take over at least some of the work, and you will liaise with him. You will continue to do your own routine work. Do not make the mistake of assuming that if the chief is away, then you must do his work for him – this course of action could lead to disaster. In any event, the chief will probably be sending in tapes to be transcribed or written instructions to be carried out. He might telephone asking for information or for something to be sent out. Watch your step here and do not thoughtlessly send an original document abroad – it may never be seen again.

You should have carefully noted both the telephone and Telex numbers of hotels and businesses on your copy of the itinerary, so you will know exactly how to contact the chief on most days of his absence, but you should think very carefully before getting in touch with him. A good general rule is to leave a travelling executive alone, except in emergencies.

Finally, be sure to make notes of everything important that happens during the chief's absence, so that when he returns you can brief him accurately and succinctly.

**Questions**

1 Your employer is to make a visit overseas. What formalities should be completed and what steps should you take before his departure to lessen the chances and minimise the consequences of (*a*) illness abroad; (*b*) loss of travel documents: (*c*) loss of cash and (*d*) loss of luggage.     (LCC PSC Office Organisation and Secretarial Procedures)

2 Having booked accommodation for your chief by telephone, it would then be necessary for you to . . .     (Pitman Secretarial Practice Intermediate)

3 For his forthcoming visit to the United States, Mr Watson (your chief) has asked you to obtain as much information as possible about the country, the companies and opportunities for developing trade with the States in the field of safety goods. List the sources you will use for this purpose and the information you are likely to obtain.     (RSA Secretarial Duties Stage II)

4 Mr Watson, your chief, has asked you to prepare a check-list of travel arrangements to be made for a visit to the United States, where he has been asked to speak at a 'Safety at Night' convention in February. Prepare a check-list for this visit.     (RSA Secretarial Duties Stage II)

5 Your chief travels abroad quite frequently. Draw up a list of books and other literature which will help you to make the travel arrangements.

# 11

# The Filing

Filing her employer's papers is one of the most important of a secretary's functions. Moreover, filing is becoming an increasingly complex and vital activity, due partly to the growing amount of paperwork which business produces, and partly to more profess-ional management which demands that decisions be based on facts – facts swiftly produced from files or records or from data-processing equipment. Therefore you should never feel that filing is beneath your dignity, or that it is something you can safely leave to an unsupervised junior.

Briefly, a filing system should fulfil three basic functions:

1  To collect in orderly fashion all the papers and documents circulating in the business
2  To preserve the material collected
3  To allow swift retrieval of the material when it is required.

A filing system can be either departmentalised or centralised, that is, either each department keeps its own files and does its own filing, or else all correspondence and documents for filing are sent to a central filing department and called for when needed. Which is the best method to follow depends on the size and nature of the business, as each method has both advantages and disadvantages.

*The advantages of a centralised filing system* are:  (*a*) greater efficiency, since specialised staff can be employed, and the whole of the filing is the responsibility of a single person; (*b*) junior staff can be trained more easily, since the whole department is engaged in filing and the various phases of the work are constantly repeated; and (*c*) a saving in staff and equipment can be made, as resources are utilised to the maximum and duplication of effort is avoided.

*The advantages of a departmental filing system* are: (*a*) if you, the secretary, do your own filing you will become so familiar with the system that you will be able to file and retrieve papers with greater speed and fewer errors. The closer proximity of the filing cabinets will speed up retrieval; (*b*) departmental filing can be done in your spare time, thereby reducing idle time and adding variety to your job; and (*c*) it is far easier to keep confidential files under lock and key with fewer pairs of eyes examining them.

There can be no doubt that most people prefer to have their current files near at hand and sometimes resist instructions to send them down to the filing department until they have well and truly finished with them.

## Classifications

Before correspondence and documents are stored away, they have to be arranged for quick and easy retrieval when needed. There are several ways of arranging or classifying documents, each of which has its own advantages and disadvantages. The method ultimately selected will depend upon the type of material to be filed, and the kind of company or organisation. The main systems are:

### Alphabetical

This is by far the most popular method, used in almost all offices, at least for correspondence. It consists in making out a file for each correspondent, and then arranging the files in strict alphabetical order. Each letter of the alphabet has its own 'Miscellaneous' file containing letters which do not warrant a separate folder. If the 'Miscellaneous' file becomes too full, it can be subdivided into several folders.

The main advantage of the alphabetical system is that it is extremely simple to manage and can be handled without any special training, providing you know your alphabet! Furthermore the contents of the folders are perfectly obvious, without any need to refer to an index.

The disadvantages are that this system does not lend itself to expansion without considerable rearrangement, there can be difficulties in adhering to a strictly alphabetical order, and there may be variations if many different people handle the files.

The only solution to this problem is to have one person only in charge of the files, and for this person to write down the rules adopted. Some companies issue written instructions on filing, but it is quite likely that you will be able to organise your own method for your own files. Decide therefore how you are going to handle every tricky situation, write down your rule, and keep to it always.

Every company has its own awkward situations and you will have to devise ways of handling them. However, some of your general rules could be the following:

1   File letters under the name of the company, not the person to whom you are writing, unless it is a purely personal correspondence.

2   If a company name contains several surnames, the first one should determine the filing position, e.g. *Smith, Klein and French* should be filed under *Smith*.

3   If you have frequent correspondence with various branches of the same company, make out a separate file for each branch, for example:

> Best Brand Plc, Manchester
> Best Brand Limited, Sydney
> Best Brand Limitada, Lisbon

4   Ignore the words *the*, *a*, *an*, as well as recurring foreign words as *Société*, *Soc. An.*, *Fratelli* or *Fr.lli*, *Firma* when they preface the actual name of the company, as they usually do.

5   File correspondence with officials of public bodies or corporations under the key word of the organisation, for example:

> London, Lord Mayor of
> Civil Engineers, Institution of
> Defence, Ministry of

6   File double-barrelled surnames under the first of the two names if they are hyphenated, but under the second name if there is no hyphen.

7   File such names as *De Quincey* and *Van Fleet* under *De* and *Van* respectively, exactly as if they were written Dequincey and Vanfleet. Such foreign names as *De Sanctis* should be treated in the same way.

8   File names beginning with *Mac*, *Mc*, *Mack* or *M'* under *Mac*.

9   File all names beginning with *S* or *St* for *Saint* under *Saint*. The same applies to French names beginning *S.* or *St.* When it comes to other languages, however, your decision should depend entirely on your familiarity with each language.

10   File all 'household words' made up of initials under the well-known word, e.g. ICI, IBM, FIAT. It is far easier to think of ICI than to remember what each initial stands for.

11   File all exotic names in strict alphabetical order, regardless of whether the first word is a given name, or Outer Mongolian for 'The'. This method may be absurd to a Mongolian but is none the less the most practical one for the non-linguist dealing with the less familiar languages.

12   Finally, and most important of all, always keep to strict alphabetical order, with *Collins* followed by *Cowper*, and then *Cullen*. If you have several Smiths, then the forenames should be in alphabetical order, e.g. *Smith, Abraham*, followed by *Smith, Benjamin*, *Smith, Charles*, and so on, until you end with *Smith, Zenobius*. In the unlikely event of your having a Smith with no initial, then this file would come first of all, followed by Smith, A., Smith, B., and Smith, C. In general, when deciding upon secondary indexing units, short comes before long, or nothing before something, for example:

> Jones
> Jones, A.
> Jones, A. A.

If personal names are identical, the order of indexing is decided by the address, for example:

> Brown, N., Birmingham
> Brown, N., Nottingham

**Numerical**

This system consists in allotting consecutive numbers to correspondents, numbering the manilla folders accordingly, and then filing them in the cabinets in numerical order. A card index is then made out giving the name of each correspondent and the allotted number. The cards are filed in alphabetical order in their box or drawer. When a file is needed, the name of the correspondent is looked up under the appropriate letter of the alphabet in the card index and the number of his file ascertained. The required file is then located in the appropriate place in the cabinet.

The advantages of the numerical system are as follows:

1   Numerical files are easier to find than alphabetically filed ones, and when a file is missing the fact is quickly spotted.
2   The file numbers can be used on letters, thereby obviating the need to refer to the card index to locate the corresponding file.
3   The system can be expanded indefinitely without disruption simply by adding new files at the back.
4   The index cards can be used for many other purposes and would probably be made out even if another filing system were used.

The single important disadvantage of the numerical system is that a file cannot usually be retrieved without first looking up its number in the card index. On the other hand, the numerical filing system can be used to great advantage, and without the need of a card index, for filing invoices, orders, cheques and other documents normally carrying consecutive numbers. (See also Terminal digit and Alphanumerical, below.)

**Geographical**

As the name implies, this system consists of grouping the files in geographical order, by country, county, territory, and so on, and then subdividing the files within each division by subject or name. This system is almost indispensable in an export office, sales department, or in any case where it is necessary to assess activities by area or territory. It is also quite popular with local authorities.

The disadvantage of the geographical system is that activities are not always carried out in a strictly geographical pattern. For instance, a salesman's territory may cover the whole of Berkshire, a part of Buckinghamshire, and a small part of Hertfordshire. The rest of Hertfordshire may be covered by another salesman, who may also deal with part of North London. Such a state of affairs would make geographical classification of their paperwork quite impractical. The solution to this difficulty is, of course, to file salesmen's papers according to territory – assuming that each salesman's territory is numbered.

Another drawback of the geographical filing system is that it requires exact knowledge of where small towns and villages are located. Constant checking has to be done and errors are easily made, especially if inexperienced people are allowed to do the filing.

**Subject**
Subject filing calls for filing material according to its subject or content. It is an extremely useful method in a number of cases. A Purchasing Office, for instance, usually files catalogues and price lists by merchandise rather than supplier's name. Thus there might be files headed 'Office Furniture', 'Office Equipment', 'Office Supplies', and so on. Each file would contain catalogues and price lists from various suppliers and so comparisons can be quickly made.

Subject files are also useful for bringing together all correspondence and papers pertaining to a recurring activity. If your employer belongs to a professional or trade association, for instance, you will want to have all matters concerning such activities in one file. The same can be said about sports activities or welfare committees within the company, and for tax matters, and so on. Authors and journalists also have subject files on the various topics in which they are interested.

The main difficulty with subject files is that it is possible to forget their existence and file papers in another file, particularly if one item of correspondence deals with more than one subject (see page 71). If you *do* decide to file some papers by subject matter, you would do well to watch this point.

**Terminal digit**
This is a variation of numerical classification and consists in arranging the files according to the last pair of digits instead of in strict

numerical order. File numbers are divided into groups of digits, such as 385.77.12; 568.18.99. All files ending in the same two digits are filed together behind a primary guide. For instance, the '12' section will contain all files ending in '12'. Within the '12' section files will be further subdivided according to the next set of digits. In this way all files ending in, say, 34.12 will be grouped together. Finally the files are arranged numerically according to the digits at the beginning of the number.

The advantage of this system is said to be that it is easier to remember two digits than a long number and consequently fewer filing errors are likely to result. Furthermore, colour coding can be used to help identify the files, if each digit is given a different colour.

The terminal digit classification is used mainly for filing punched cards and in other cases where vast quantities of identical pieces have to be filed. It would not be considered for straightforward correspondence filing!


### Decimal

The best known, but by no means the only, decimal filing system is the Dewey Decimal system, so called after its originator, Dr Melvil Dewey. Dr Dewey devised the system for his own library, New York State Library in Albany, New York, and it was gradually adopted by all US libraries and many others throughout the world.

The Dewey classification regards all knowledge as unity which can be divided into nine classes. Works which are too general to be included in any of them form a tenth class. The classes are numbered from 0 to 9, as follows:

| | | | |
|---|---|---|---|
| 0 | General Works | 5 | Natural Science |
| 1 | Philosophy | 6 | Useful Arts |
| 2 | Religion | 7 | Fine Arts |
| 3 | Sociology | 8 | Literature |
| 4 | Philology | 9 | History |

Each class is separated into nine divisions, except 'General Works, which has no divisions. The second digit therefore corresponds to a division. If we take 'Fine Arts', for instance, which is classified as '7', we will find that it is subdivided into:

710 Landscape Gardening
720 Architecture
730 Sculpture
740 Drawing, Decoration and Design

and so on.

Each of these divisions can be further subdivided into nine sections, each of which can in turn be subdivided into nine subsections. In each subdivision a further digit is added by way of identification.

The Dewey Decimal System obviously requires an index. In fact libraries usually have two: a Subject Index and an Author Index. If you know the title of the book but not its author, you go to the Subject Index, look up the title, note the code number of the book, and incidentally also the name of its author, then locate the volume on the library shelves. The books are, of course, set out on the shelves in numerical order, so that all the books in one class are together.

The development of the Dewey Decimal system of classification was a boon to libraries all over the world, many of which were badly classified or not classified at all. Nowadays, many libraries have their indexes on microfiches, which we shall deal with later in this chapter. The Dewey Decimal system is quite suitable for business filing, and is worth considering in appropriate cases.

**Alphanumerical**

As the name implies, this system is a combination of the numerical and the alphabetical classification. Each letter of the alphabet is allocated a number, for instance A is 1, B is 2, C is 3, and so on. Each file opened within a group is numbered consecutively: 1/1, 1/2, 1/3, 1/4, and so on. The files are then arranged alphabetically in the cabinet and the numbers are simply used as a reference on correspondence.

Another alphanumerical system calls for the files to be arranged in alphabetical groups, and numbered within each group. Each letter, or part of a letter, has a guide card with an index of the numbered files within that group. The first guide card, covering for instance the group Aa-Am would be numbered A.1 and the first file to be opened in that group, e.g. Alden and Company Plc, would be numbered A(1)1. The next file to be opened, Addis, H. V., would be numbered A(1)2 and placed next to the previous one. The third file, say Anders, W. G., would be numbered A(1)3 and would go after Addis. Strict alphabetical order is not followed in this system: all names between Aa and Am, for instance, are given a consecutive number in the order in which they are opened. Although they are rather elaborate, the alphanumerical systems are more accurate than purely alphabetical ones.

## Storage

There are a number of different ways in which files can be stored and your choice of method will depend on such factors as:

1   the type of business of your company,
2   the type and size of the papers you will be filing, e.g. correspon-
    dence, legal documents, plans and drawings,
3   the amount of material to be filed,
4   the frequency with which the material will be needed,
5   the classification method used.

These are the main storage methods available:

**Horizontal**   This method consists in filing the material flat, one paper on top of the other, in drawers or on shelves. It is a method which generally has little to recommend it, since material filed in this way takes up a considerable amount of space and is difficult to retrieve. It is useful, however, for architectural drawings, or very large books and ledgers.

**Vertical**   When material is stored vertically, the papers are put in a card folder, with a tab or protruding edge at the broadest side, on which the code or an indication of the contents can be written. The folders are then filed one behind the other in filing cabinets, sometimes with divider cards to subdivide the groups of folders for ease of retrieval (see Fig. 11.1).

**Suspended**   This is another form of vertical filing, when the individual folders are inserted in pockets suspended in the cabinet drawers. There are many different models to choose from, all of them with some form of identification tab (see Fig. 11.2)

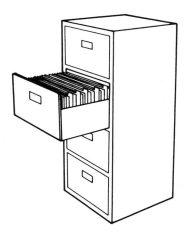

**Fig. 11.1**   A cabinet using a vertical filing system

**Lateral**   Here the files are stored laterally, one beside the other, in suspended cradles in filing cupboards. Many different models are on the market and they can also be built-in (see Fig. 11.3). The lateral storage method has a slight advantage where numerical classification is used, since it enables all the numbers to be seen clearly at a glance.

**Microfilming**   Microfilming is a way of keeping the information without keeping the paper. Documents are photographed and greatly reduced in size on the film, thereby saving considerable space. The documents photographed are then frequently destroyed. The negatives can be stored in one of the following ways, partly depending on the type of film used for taking the photographs: in rolls; on sheets known as microfiches; in transparent jackets into which strips of the film are inserted; in an ordinary record card, in which an aperture is cut to house a strip of film; or in data-processing cards, into which a single frame of the film is mounted.

Microfilm can also be produced directly from computer processed information. This is known as Computer Originated Microfilm or Computer Output Microfilm (COM). When the filmed material is to be consulted, the negative is placed in a microreader which magnifies sufficiently for easy reading.

**Fig. 11.2**　Suspension pockets (Expandex Ltd)

The great advantage of microfilming is the enormous amount of space it can save. It can also result in savings of time and labour by cutting out the need to copy out documents. A further advantage is that by filming important documents, such as plans and drawings, the originals can be kept safely out of harm's way and will not be torn and endangered by frequent handling.

As you will appreciate, a microfilming programme is only as good as its index system. If you do not know where to find a required negative swiftly on demand, then the whole system will be a failure.

**Automatic filing**　Several automatic methods have been devised for filing, and particularly for retrieval. They range from push-button selection of a particular shelf, to electronic retrieval of a single file. With the Minitrieve system you simply touch the file number digits on the keyboard, then push the 'Retrieve' button.

**Fig. 11.3** A filing cupboard with lateral files (Expandex Ltd)

The file will then be delivered to you automatically. To send it 'home', you simply push the 'Restore' button.

**Computerised storage of information** Probably the most automatic form of filing is computerised storage of information, also known as electronic filing. You can file away a letter or a document which you have just typed on your word processor simply by pressing one of the keys. The discs on which the letters or reports have been typed can then be filed away for retrieval and re-use later on. This type of storage also requires an index, as you will realise. The British Telecom electronic mail service mentioned in Chapter 4 also includes an electronic filing option.

## How to do the filing

Regardless of the classification system used, and whether your company has a centralised or decentralised filing operation, you will certainly have to get down to it at some time, and a little planning will save you time and effort. Throughout your working day you will have accumulated papers for filing in your filing tray. Now clear the decks, and empty it out, then proceed as follows:

1   First of all divide your filing into broad categories, i.e. correspondence, folders and catalogues, invoices, bills, and so on, separating out any material needing a new folder.

2   Take a red crayon and underline the name under which the paper is to be filed. If using a numerical system, look up the appropriate file number in your card index and write it on the paper. Make sure you are not led astray by working 'automatically'. The Berkshire representative may write in from the Hotel Bristol in Edinburgh, but you will not want to file his letter under 'Bristol, Hotel'.

3   If you have not already done so, staple every carbon to the incoming letter to which it refers. Never use paper clips or pins in filing. They add unnecessary bulk to the folders, and other papers get caught in them.

4   Make a red crayon line in the margin against the salient point in each letter. This will facilitate matters later on when you are instructed to find the letter in which Bloggs and Company offered 10 000 carpet tacks at £2 per thousand!

5   Carefully mend any tears in the letters with Sellotape and fold any document which is too big to go into the file, unless it should not be folded.

6   If you have a large number of documents to be filed alphabetically, arrange them first by using a letter sorter. You can use a so-called concertina file, which is a wallet-folder with the letters of the alphabet protruding on tabs, or you can devise a sorter of your own.

7   If you have a great many papers to file in numerical order, start off by dividing them into groups. First put all the thousands

together, then put each pile of thousands into their respective
hundreds, then into tens, and finally into exact numerical order.

8  Make out, or open up as they say in offices, any new file that is
needed. Write in a clear bold hand or, if you are typing the labels,
use capital letters.

You are now ready to file your papers in the cabinets or the
suspension files. Always take the papers to the file, and not vice
versa. Make a point of taking out the whole file rather than
attempting to slide a paper into it. This method prevents many filing
errors. Make a habit of lifting out a file with both hands, rather than
plucking it out by the tab.

Folders should never be overfull. If the one you are handling is
stuffed full, and difficult to handle, take the opportunity to open a
new one for the more recent material. Deal similarly with the
miscellaneous files; do not let them get out of hand. As soon as you
have several letters to one correspondent, open up a new file and
thereby thin down the miscellaneous file.

If you have several letters or other papers for one file, make sure
you put them in the folder in chronological order, that is, first the
oldest letter, then the rest in chronological order, ending with the
most recent.

## Cross-referencing

It sometimes happens that material on one subject is to be found in
more than one file. For instance, material on a new product may be
in a 'Product File', but if a licensing agreement for the manufacture
of that product is granted to an overseas firm, for instance, another
file will be opened in the name of the licensee. In such a case, the
'Product File' would be marked 'See also correspondence in File X'.
Likewise, File X would be marked 'See also Product File'. This
exercise, known as cross-referencing, saves the trouble of making
two copies of the relevant correspondence and it also ensures that
no vital information is overlooked by someone who does not realise
that there are two files on closely-related subjects. Cross-
referencing also occurs in indexing, as we shall see later.

## Loaning out a file

Never take out a single document or letter from a file for someone to peruse. If the chief asks for a letter, send in the whole file, with a marker indicating where the wanted letter is to be found. These markers, variously known as tabs or indicators, come in a number of forms. They can be tiny metal gadgets, in various colours, which clip at the top of a document and stick out above the file, or they can look like bookmarks. You can also quite simply use several strips of sticky paper protruding from the file and marked, for instance, 'Bloggs' letter of 11/4/8–', 'Our reply of 30/4/8–' and so on. In this way the chief will have the whole story flagged out for him.

Having removed a file from the cabinet, you will need a system to remind you who has it, and when it was borrowed. A common method is to use an 'Out' card. Inserted in place of the file, it will tell you immediately that the file has been borrowed. The 'Out' card should give the name or number of the file, the name of the borrower, the date on which it was borrowed, and a space for the date when it is returned. In this way, if someone else should ask for the file, you will know exactly who has it (see Fig. 11.4).

| **OUT** | | | |
|---|---|---|---|
| Date taken | Folder number or name | Taken by | Date returned |
| . . . . . . | . . . . . . . . . . . . . | . . . . . . | . . . . . . |
| . . . . . . | . . . . . . . . . . . . . | . . . . . . | . . . . . . |
| . . . . . . | . . . . . . . . . . . . . | . . . . . . | . . . . . . |
| . . . . . . | . . . . . . . . . . . . . | . . . . . . | . . . . . . |
| . . . . . . | . . . . . . . . . . . . . | . . . . . . | . . . . . . |

**Fig. 11.4**   An OUT card

An even better method is to have a suspended 'absent' wallet, which enables you not only to give details of the whereabouts of the missing file, but also to store any new papers belonging to it.

**Colour coding**
If your 'Out' cards are in a bright, distinct colour you will be able to see at a glance which files are on loan, and thereby check up on those people who tend to keep files long after they need them.

Colour also serves other purposes, mainly in aiding rapid retrieval. In geographical filing, for instance, you can use a different colour folder for each country or county and, if you feel this would help you to find a file more quickly, you could have suppliers' files in one colour, customers' in another, and so on.

## Follow-up systems

Quite frequently a letter or document has to be followed up, or 'brought forward' for action at a later date. If, for instance, a correspondent has been promised an answer which requires some research, a preliminary reply is sent off straight away with a promise of a full answer later on.

In such cases, file the correspondence in the usual way, but make a note of the file number, subject and date of the original letter in your diary under the date when you expect the full reply to become available. On that date remove the file from the cabinet and place it before your chief, with an explanatory note, if necessary, and, needless to say, the additional information, if it has arrived on your desk.

If your job involves many items of this nature and your diary begins to get cluttered with B/F (brought forward) notes, then you should consider having a separate diary for these entries. Alternatively you can keep all correspondence needing further action in a separate file, to be gone through daily. This is not usually a good idea, however, since it keeps the correspondence out of the file where it belongs, and involves you in a daily search through the Pending File. There is a legitimate role for the latter, as we shall see.

**The 'tickler' file**
Here you have the perfect follow-up system. Set aside twelve pockets in your filing cabinet drawer and label them from January to

December. Have an inner file with compartments inside the pocket pertaining to the current month, labelling them from 1 to 28, 1 to 30 or 1 to 31 as appropriate.

You then take an extra carbon, on a different coloured paper, of any letter which will need following up or which requires action to be taken later. Place all 'tickler' carbons in the appropriate month, or if they are to be followed up in the current month, then in the appropriate date compartment. At the beginning of every month you divide the 'ticklers' into their appropriate dates, and move the folder into the current month pocket.

Every morning you should take a look into the day's 'tickler' file, take out all carbons or other reminders from it, and place them on the chief's desk with a note, or, where appropriate, write a follow-up letter yourself.

Enlist your chief's cooperation by asking him to note on the 'tickler' carbon when he wants the letter followed-up. If you leave the 'ticklers' behind the letters when they go in for signature, it is no trouble for the chief to scribble the appropriate date on them.

Apart from carbons, the 'tickler' file can house reminders of the innumerable tasks which have to be carried out at regular intervals, monthly, weekly or even half-yearly. The same applies to reports or articles to be written and plans or programmes to be prepared, but do give yourself and the chief plenty of time. If, for instance, a report is needed by 31 March, have a reminder on 15 March, then again on 20 March, on 25 March and on 30 March. As you come to the reminders you can throw them out if you know the chief is attending to the task. If not, a gentle reminder from you would be in order.

## Pending files

A pending file is usually made out for matters which cannot be dealt with immediately. It can be arranged in the same way as other files, either alphabetically, by subject matter or in any other suitable way. A pending file should be made out only when absolutely necessary and should not be used as an excuse to procrastinate. Examples of genuine reasons for opening a pending file are: (*a*) if the chief is away on a business trip and has instructed you to hold any correspondence on a given matter until his return; (*b*) when comments are expected on a subject from a number of people; (*c*) if an advertisement has been placed and replies are to be kept until no more can be expected.

## Indexes

If you are using a numerical filing system, an index is essential, as we have seen. The index can take many forms, such as:

*A strip index* This simply consists of strips containing the basic information, namely name and number of file, inserted into a board. All the strips on a board are visible at a glance and the strips are easily removable (see Fig. 11.5).

*A visible index* This consists of larger cards, which can therefore hold more information, cut away at the bottom to reveal the essential name and file number, so that here too a whole batch of file names and numbers can be seen at a glance (see Fig. 11.6).

**Fig. 11.5** A T-card and strip index system (Cumbermay Ltd)

**Fig. 11.6**   A visible index (Expandex Ltd)

*A card index*   Here the required information is simply typed on cards, which are then kept in anything from a small plastic box, with suitable dividers, to drawers. Both the cards and the boxes obviously come in different sizes and the cards can also be accommodated in wheels which rotate around a spindle. Other variations on this theme are available to suit all requirements (see Fig. 11.7)

Much more important is the use you make of your card index, for it can be one of the secretary's most valuable tools, not only for her own use, but in keeping track of the employer's contacts.

Write the name of the company, or the surname in the case of an individual, right at the top of the card, well to the left. Type the file number on the far right, or if you do not use a numerical filing system, reserve this place for the telephone number, complete with dialling code.

If you file alphabetically and there is room for doubt as to where a company's folder is filed, then type in 'Filed under So-and-So'. For instance, British Olivetti should strictly be filed under 'British', but nine times out of ten your chief will ask for the Olivetti file. So have a card headed OLIVETTI, and type underneath 'Filed under British Olivetti'.

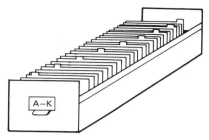

**Fig. 11.7**   A card index

Exactly beneath the name of the company, repeat it in full, giving initials and full style, for instance:

GRANT          56
W. S. Grant Plc

Follow this with the full postal address, complete with postcode and telephone number. If the company has several addresses and you deal with all of them, give each one, together with the names and correct initials of the executives concerned.

If you deal with several executives at the same address, then list all their names in full, as well as their positions. Add any other useful information, such as the name or nickname by which the person concerned is known to your chief, or such useful intelligence as 'Secretary of Such-and-Such Society', 'no connection with So-and-So's of Leeds', or 'formerly Catkins & Sons Ltd'. You will also find it useful to add in parentheses the name of the executives' secretaries and their assistants if you deal with them from time to time. All this information serves to make your work easier and helps you to understand what is going on and, in many cases, why.

Other items of intelligence can be typed in at appropriate times. Addresses of new branches, newcomers to the company, promotions and mergers can all usefully be recorded on the cards. Temporary arrangements, such as the annual factory closedown, can be added in pencil.

## Safety and confidentiality

You already know how important your employer's papers are, so you should not need to be told that they should be kept in a sheltered place, away from excessive heat, humidity, or light. Indeed, if you file all material entrusted to your care in the cabinets or cupboards provided, promptly and conscientiously, they will no doubt be preserved in good condition. Do, however, bear in mind that photographs, drawings and plans deteriorate if exposed to sunlight, so put them away without delay.

Some files also have to be kept away from prying eyes. These are the confidential files, such as the personnel files or those containing details of salaries, new inventions, figures on turnover, profit, and so on. Companies will vary in what they consider confidential, but your employer will certainly put you in the picture.

Confidential files should be kept in a cabinet drawer, or cupboard which can be locked and you must unfailingly lock up every afternoon before leaving the office, and take the key with you. You should not allow anyone to poke around in your filing cabinet. Should an executive other than your own chief ask for a file which you suspect is confidential, check with your chief before handing it over.

## Files and their life cycle

If you kept every file indefinitely, you would soon be so hemmed in by paper that you could hardly get into your office. A system therefore has to be devised to destroy those papers which are no longer required. Different companies have different ways of handling this problem and the individual secretary obviously has to fall in with the system advocated by the employer.

One excellent system, however, is to allow the company's filing to move through three stages corresponding to the gradual decline in usefulness of a paper during the course of its life.

**The active files.**  All papers would start off in the active files, which should be located as near as possible to the person using them, preferably in a deep filing drawer in his or her desk. At this stage papers would be in constant use, and having them near at hand would save time and effort.

**The semi-active files**  Once a business transaction is completed papers pertaining to it are only needed very infrequently, if at all, and there is no further point in having them in one's desk taking up valuable space. All such papers are therefore transferred to the semi-active files, located preferably somewhere in the department, in the care of a filing clerk.

**The inactive files.** The semi-active files are gone through, or 'thinned' at regular intervals, preferably every year, and all unnecessary papers removed and destroyed. General correspondence should not need to be referred to after a year or eighteen months, and can therefore safely be destroyed. Invoices should be retained for six years, as should any papers which might be needed for Income Tax purposes. Insurance policies should be retained so long as they are in force. Title deeds and other important documents should be retained indefinitely. This remaining material is vitally important, but will not be needed very often, and can therefore be relegated to a central location.

If this system is used, papers which are frequently needed are always nearby, while everything which has ceased to be of value is destroyed, and not left to occupy unnecessary space. If you have many papers to destroy, or if some confidentiality is still needed even at that stage, shredding machines are available to do the job for you.

**Questions**
1 Describe how you would use the following: (*a*) index card; (*b*) absent card; (*c*) cross reference card; and (*d*) strip index.     (Pitman Secretarial Practice Intermediate)
2 For the January management meeting at Head Office, all the company's managers have been asked to be prepared to discuss proposals for a unified filing system to be adopted throughout the company. At present your section in Hampshire uses numerical filing and Mr Watson (your chief) wants you to list briefly in a memorandum, the advantages and disadvantages of your numerical method of filing, so that he can discuss these points at the meeting.     (RSA Secretarial Duties Stage II)
3 Mr Watson (your chief) has been made aware that certain items of correspondence have been taken from the files and often mislaid, causing delays when urgently required. He wants to ensure that if there is a unified system for the company attention is paid to control of absent files. Briefly outline for him, in a memorandum, a suggested method to ensure that a procedure

is followed to safeguard the borrowing of files.    (RSA Secretarial Duties Stage II)

4  Select four of the following items and describe the filing equipment which would best suit each one: (*a*) maps and large plans; (*b*) used ink stencils; (*c*) catalogues and pamphlets; (*d*) invoices; (*e*) weekly pay-roll sheets; (*f*) personnel record cards.    (LCC PSC Office Organisation and Secretarial Procedures)

5  List and discuss the essential steps necessary to devise and operate a successful departmental filing system.    (LCC PSC Office Organisation and Secretarial Procedures)

6  What do you understand by microfilming?

7  How would you use colour to help in the rapid retrieval of files?

8  What is the purpose of a 'Pending File'?

9  A card index can be one of the secretary's most valuable tools. Give two of its uses.

10  Confidential files have to be protected from prying eyes and unofficial use. Where would you keep them, and what steps would you take to protect them?

# 12

# Figure Work

The amount of figure work a secretary is called upon to do varies from none at all to a considerable amount. Some secretaries act as book-keeper, paymistress and statistician, with occasional research work thrown in for good measure. It is, therefore, always wise to find out exactly what is expected before taking on a job, especially if extensive figure work does not appeal to you.

## Methods of payment

A number of methods are used by businesses to pay for the goods and services they need and for the everyday running of the operation.

**Cash**  Cash is frequently used for the payment of wages and always for the small casual expenses necessary for the day-to-day running of the business. The secretary is usually responsible for the petty cash account, as we shall see later. Coins and notes can be sent through the post, but should always be registered.

**Cash on delivery** (COD)  Goods sent COD are paid for by the recipient, to the postman when he delivers the parcel. The sender must fill in the Despatch Document and special address label provided by the Post Office, pay the COD fee, and hand in the package at the counter.

**Stamps**  Postage stamps are commonly used for the payment of brochures, booklets, or other printed matter ordered by post.

**Postal orders**   Postal orders can be purchased from the Post Office for amounts ranging from 25p to £10. The value can be increased by affixing one or two unused stamps up to the value of 4½p in the spaces provided on the order. In addition, a fee is charged for each order. The sender then fills in the payee's name, and the name of the office of payment, or the name of the town, village or district where the payee lives. The postal order will then be payable in any post office in the place named. Alternatively, the postal order may be crossed and it is then only payable through a bank. Each postal order has a counterfoil and it is wise to fill it in and keep it as a record. Some other countries cash British postal orders, and even issue them, and there is a list of these countries in the *Post Office Guide*. Postal orders are useful to pay for small items ordered by mail, but they are not in common use in business.

**Cheques**   These are the most common form of payment used in business. Full details follow later in this chapter.

**National Giro**   Girobank cheques can be used exactly like other bank cheques to pay for goods or services. In addition, a Girobank account holder can transfer money from his account to that of another account holder, by using a transfer form instead of a cheque. Companies or individuals who do not have a Girobank account can make cash payments to account holders at any post office by using the standard Girobank Transcash Form G 20, and paying the corresponding fee. Many bills for electricity, gas, telephone, etc., already have a Girobank transfer form attached, and many people use this convenient way to pay their bills.

**Credit transfer**.   According to a survey recently carried out by Western Trust and Savings, 63 per cent of employees in the UK have their salary paid into a bank account. This method has advantages both for the employee and for the employer: for the employee it means, among other things, safety from being mugged on the way home with a fat paypacket in his pocket, and for the employer it greatly simplifies the paying out of salaries. Instead of drawing a cheque for each employee, the employer draws one cheque covering the total amount to be paid. He then sends the cheque to his bank, together with a list of the employees to be paid, the amount due, and the name and branch of their banks. The amounts to be paid are then transferred directly into the employee's account.

**Standing orders**   A client can instruct his bank to pay certain sums periodically from his current account to another person or business. The bank is given the name and bank of the payee, the amount to be paid, and the date on which payment is to be made. The bank then automatically makes the payment until the order is stopped. Standing orders are a very useful way of paying mortgages, insurance premiums, subscriptions to periodicals, and other regularly recurring expenses. Having giving the order, the client no longer has to bother remembering to make payment, writing out cheques, and so on.

**Direct debit**   This is similar to a standing order, but with a very important difference in that it involves authorising a company to debit your bank account for a *variable* sum at regular intervals. At first only insurance companies required this type of payment, but now it is becoming widespread. As the amount involved is variable, the customer has not got quite the same control as with a standing order although there are strict safeguards.

**Credit cards**   We saw in Chapter 10 how useful credit cards can be when travelling: meals, airline tickets and even cash, up to a stipulated amount, can be obtained simply by producing a plastic card. The credit card holder is then billed at the end of the month, and can pay for all the purchases with only one cheque. Better still, if he pays the bill right away, the service is free of charge. Credit cards can also be used when ordering goods by mail, or indeed by computer, and mail-order houses do a lot of business in this way.

**Bank cash cards**   If you have a bank account, you can apply for a cash card. It enables you to obtain cash from the dispensers situated outside many of the bank's branches. Some of these machines provide other everyday banking services, so that you can check the balance of your account, or ask for a new cheque book or a detailed statement to be sent to your home.

**Bank cheque cards**   A cheque guarantee card is not a credit card, but, as its name implies, will guarantee your cheques for all payments up to the value of £50. Some cards, such as the Barclaycard, combine the functions of the credit card and the cheque guarantee card.

**Documentary credit**   Companies which buy goods from abroad often pay for them by documentary credit or Letter of Credit (L/C), as mentioned in Chapter 1. The money is paid to the supplier's bank, which does not release it until the supplier produces the invoice and shipping documents to prove that the goods have been despatched. In this way both buyer and seller are protected: the buyer knows the bank will not release the money without proof of shipment, and the seller knows the money is actually there, and will be handed over as soon as he has despatched the goods.

**Bills of exchange**   These were also mentioned in Chapter 1. They are mainly used in the export/import business. A completes the Bill, stating how much B is to pay, and on what date. He signs it and sends it to B, who signs it in turn, to signify his agreement to pay the amount stated when the bill matures, that is, when the payment date is reached. Bills are usually payable 'at sight', that is immediately on presentation, at 30, 60, 90 or 180 days. The number of days may be agreed to coincide with shipping dates, or as a means of giving credit to the buyer.

**Telegraphic transfer**   Sums of money can be transferred abroad very swiftly and easily by telegraphic transfer, simply by instructing your bank. Although they are still called telegraphic transfers, nowadays the instructions are given mainly by Telex.

**SWIFT**   This is a computer-based transfer system. It was developed by the Society for Worldwide Interbank Financial Telecommunications (SWIFT), hence its name. It is very simple indeed to use. Suppose that a buyer in the UK wants to make a payment to a supplier in Milan. He simply informs his bank, and makes the necessary amount of money available from his current account. The bank then contacts its nearest SWIFT member bank, which makes the transfer by computer to the nearest Italian member bank. The whole transaction can be completed within the space of half an hour. SWIFT is available in the UK, the rest of Europe, the USA, Canada, Australia, Japan, Latin America, South Africa, Singapore, Hong Kong, Israel and New Zealand. The remaining countries will no doubt be connected before long.

# Bank accounts

Basically, two types of account can be opened with a bank: a deposit account and a current account.

### Deposit account

This is the type of account in which the customer deposits his surplus cash with a view to earning interest on it. Cheques, postal orders and cash can all be paid into a deposit account, and the amounts are entered on a paying-in slip provided by the bank. The bank reserves the right to ask the customer for several days' notice of withdrawal, but in practice seldom does so. Withdrawals are made by filling in a withdrawal form. A statement of account is sent to the customer as requested, usually either monthly or quarterly.

### Current account

A current account is an account from which bills can be paid and money withdrawn by means of cheques. Very few banks pay interest on current accounts, but a charge is made at intervals. This is variously called a 'bank charge', a 'commission', or a 'ledger fee', and is usually waived if the balance of the account does not fall below a certain level.

Payments into the account are made by means of paying-in slips and a statement is sent to customers at any interval required. If you are put in charge of your chief's current account, you would be well advised to request a monthly statement.

Like the deposit account, the current account can be opened either in the name of a single company or individual, or jointly in the name of two people, whether husband and wife or business partners. The arrangements for operating the account are stipulated by the customer. In the case of two business partners, for instance, they may decide that both signatures should appear on cheques. They inform the bank accordingly, and the bank will consequently only honour cheques which have both signatures. When a current account is opened, the bank asks for a specimen signature of the person or persons who will be signing the cheques, and these signatures are kept for reference.

## Making out cheques

Cheques are supplied in books, usually with a counterfoil. All you have to do to make out a cheque is to complete a cheque form with the necessary details, which you also write on the counterfoil. In the top right-hand corner is a space for the date. Take care to get it right, as banks will not process cheques which are dated ahead, nor which are more than six months old.

**Payee**   This is the person or company to whom the money is to be paid. Write the payee's name against the word 'Pay'. Here again be careful to get the name right and to include initials, Plc or whatever the full style is. If you are drawing money for yourself (out of your own bank account, of course!) then you write 'Cash' or 'Self' on the payee line.

**Amount**   The amount is written in words on the line beneath the payee, but only the whole number of pounds should be spelt out, with the pence following in figures. You would write, for instance: Twenty pounds 20p. If there were no pence, then you would write: Twenty pounds only. The amount is repeated, in figures this time, in the small box on the right. Make sure that both words and figures correspond and are absolutely clear, and that you do not leave any spaces in which a person could fraudulently add a word or a digit.

**Signature**   Cheques are signed in the bottom right-hand corner. As we have seen, sometimes two signatures are required.

**Counterfoil**   When writing out a cheque, fill in the details on the counterfoil at the same time. This is very important in providing a convenient record of how much money there is left in the account and will also help in checking the bank statement.

## Crossed and open cheques

There are two types of cheque: crossed or open. The crossed cheque is so called because it has two parallel lines across it, while the open cheque has not. The difference is that a crossed cheque cannot be cashed over the counter at a bank, but must be paid into an account. An open cheque can be cashed over the counter at the branch of the bank on which it is drawn.

Should a crossed cheque falls into the hands of an unauthorised person, he could not cash it but would have to deposit it in a bank account and the bank would therefore be able to trace him. On the other hand, if an open cheque is cashed over the counter by an unauthorised person, the money is seldom recovered.

For this reason it is always prudent to use crossed cheques for paying bills or sending money through the post. Books of cheques are available either crossed or open. If, however, you want to cross an open cheque before mailing it you can do so by drawing two parallel lines in ink across it. To open a crossed cheque to draw cash for yourself at your own branch, simply write 'Pay cash' between the parallel lines and add your signature underneath.

**Special crossings**
If you want to stipulate that a cheque be cashed at a certain branch of a certain bank, then write the name of the bank and branch inside the crossing, as shown in Fig. 12.1a.

If you want to take an extra precaution against fraud, you can write 'Under £20', for instance, inside the crossing of a cheque made out for £10. This would ensure that no one could alter the £10 to £100 by adding a nought. This type of crossing is often used when ordering theatre tickets with a blank cheque. (See Fig. 12.1b.)

Another kind of crossing, used for paying telephone bills and the like, is the insertion of the words 'A/c Payee only' between the lines

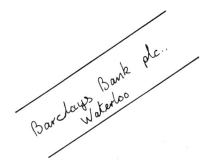

**Fig. 12.1a**  A cheque crossing to specify the branch at which it can be encashed

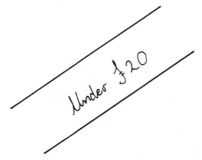

**Fig. 12.1b**    A cheque crossing to prevent the amount being fraudulently
increased

of the crossing. In this way the cheque can only be paid into the
account of the person or company to whom it is made out.

## Stopping payment

If you should lose your cheque book, a cheque sent through the post
has gone astray, or you decide to stop payment on a cheque, you
should inform the bank manager at once. He will want to know the
number, date and amount of the cheque, as well as the payee's
name. You should then confirm these details in writing, either by
letter or on the appropriate form provided by the bank.

Provided you are in time, the bank will stop payment, and if the
cheque is presented later it will be returned unpaid. When a bank
has accepted instructions to stop payment on a lost cheque it is quite
safe to issue a duplicate to the original payee. However, once a
cheque has a cheque card number on the back, it cannot be stopped.

### Stale cheques

Cheques are valid for six months from the date they are made out.
After that they are not usually accepted for payment by the bank.

### 'Refer to Drawer' cheques

If a cheque is presented for payment and there is not sufficient
money in the account to cover it, it is returned to the payee's bank
marked R/D – 'refer to drawer'. The payee then has to contact the
drawer of the cheque to obtain payment. Cheques can be returned

for other reasons, for example if they are not made out correctly, but the most common reason by far is insufficiency of funds.

**Blank cheques**
A blank cheque is one which is complete in every detail except the amount, which is meant to be filled in by the payee. Every authority, including your own common sense, will advise you against ever making out such a cheque, since you, the drawer, have no control over the amount the payee might fill in. In spite of this, theatres are constantly urging people to write out blank cheques for tickets with a crossing limiting the amount, as we saw previously. Do always remain aware of the dangers in issuing blank cheques.

# Paying into an account

Cheques received from others must be paid into the account to enable the bank to collect the amounts and credit the account accordingly. Enter the details of the cheques on a paying-in slip and hand both cheques and slip, together with any cash, to the bank cashier.

There are two types of paying-in slip. One is for paying amounts in at the branch where the account is kept; the other is for paying in at any other branch. Slips are supplied in book form, with a counterfoil. You should, of course, always fill in the counterfoil as well, as it is a useful record of all sums paid in.

When the cashier has checked the amounts handed in, he will stamp the credit slip and counterfoil and initial them as a receipt. The book of paying-in slips is then returned to you.

When paying in cheques it is not necessary to endorse them, i.e. to sign them on the back. If, however, you use a cheque made out to you to make a payment to someone else, then you must sign it on the back before handing it over. The signature must correspond exactly with the name shown on the face of the cheque. If the cheque is made out to Mary F. Brown, for instance, then it must be endorsed Mary F. Brown on the back. If the cheque is made out to 'The Secretary, Windsmoore Sports Club', then it should be endorsed with the secretary's usual signature, followed by 'Secretary, Windsmoore Sports Club'.

# The bank statement

The holder of a current account is sent a bank statement as often as required, but usually monthly or when a page is full, whichever occurs first. You can, however, have a statement sent at any time, and can also ask for the balance over the counter at the bank.

The accounting and recording work in banks is done mainly by computer these days. Cheques that have been paid are identified on the statement by their serial number. Other payments from, and credits into the account, are identified by symbols which are explained in a key printed on the statement.

### The reconciliation statement

You should always check the entries on the bank statement against the entries on the counterfoils of the cheque book and paying-in book. Even so, the balance shown on the bank statement will seldom agree exactly with your own figures, for one or more of the following reasons:

1  Some of the cheques you have made out may not yet have been presented for payment;
2  Standing order payments and direct debits may have been made, but not yet recorded;
3  Bank charges may have been debited from the account, but not yet recorded;
4  Some cheques paid in to the bank may not yet have been credited.

Once you have checked the entries on the bank statement against the counterfoils of the cheque book and paying-in book, ticking each off methodically, you should proceed as follows. List outstanding cheques, that is, those which have not yet been presented for payment, and also list credits outstanding, that is, sums paid into the bank but not yet credited. Enter as payments any standing orders or direct debits, as well as bank charges, and allow for any receipts or dividends received by the bank direct. Then prepare a reconciliation statement as shown in Fig. 12.2.

If you check the account in this way every month, you can give the chief a correct statement of his bank balance at any moment, simply by making a quick reference to the cheque book and paying-in

```
Balance shown on Bank Statement of account
  2 March 19--                                          2 260.90

  Deduct cheques not presented

  1270  Brown, Scott & Marshall     5.00
  1271  Gresham, Plc               20.50
  1272  The Glass Company           3.96
  1273  Herbert Welsh             190.75

  Deduct standing orders
  Phoenix Insurance Co.            25.00
  FIPA dues                         8.00                  253.21
                                   ------
                                                        2 007.69

  Add cheques not credited

  Guest                           323.50
  Swift                            25.00                  348.50
                                   ------
         Cash balance should be                        £2 356.19
```

**Fig. 12.2** A bank reconciliation statement

book. Mark the counterfoil of the last cheque included in the reconciliation statement, and similarly in the paying-in book. Note any cheques which have been outstanding for some time. When a cheque has been outstanding for more than a month, it is advisable to get in touch with the payee to discover why. A cheque lapses after six months.

## Other bank services

Banks provide a number of other services, some of which have been described in other chapters. We shall mention just one more here, as it is particularly relevant to business, namely *loans*.

A bank can lend a customer money in two ways:

1 By making an agreed sum of money available for a definite period, at the end of which the principal, that is, the sum borrowed will be returned, together with an agreed interest. This arrangement is known as a *bank loan*.

2 By permitting the customer to overdraw on his account. This means that although the customer has insufficient money in his current account he is allowed to continue drawing cheques up to an agreed amount. This arrangement is known as an *overdraft* and, of course, there is a charge to pay for this facility which is normally higher than the interest rate on a bank loan.

## The petty cash book

The secretary frequently has responsibility for the petty cash. Quite simply, you are allocated a sum, known as a *float*, either once a month or once a week, to cover small incidental expenses, and you are held responsible for taking care of it, and recording how it was spent.

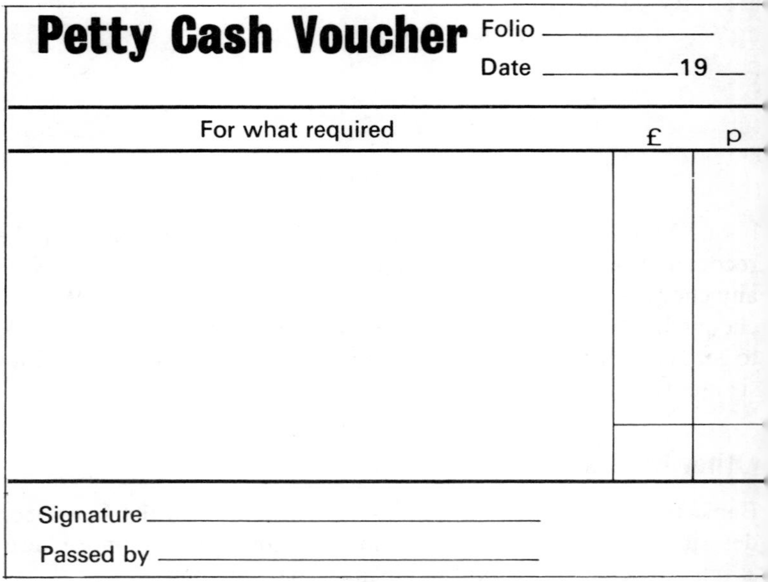

| Petty Cash Voucher | Folio _____ Date _____ 19 __ | | |
|---|---|---|---|
| For what required | | £ | p |
| | | | |
| | | | |
| | | | |
| | | | |
| | | | |
| Signature _____ | | | |
| Passed by _____ | | | |

**Fig. 12.3**   Petty Cash voucher

Expenditures which frequently come out of petty cash include bus fares if you or other office employees go on an errand for the company, a small supply of stamps for urgent letters, emergency purchases of stationery or other small items, tips to messengers, milk and tea, fees for window cleaning, or other services.

Since every small outlay has to be accounted for to ensure a balance in the petty cash book, you should make out a petty cash voucher every time money is drawn out of the box. Wherever possible every voucher should be supported by a receipt, but obviously this is impractical in every instance.

If you pay the window cleaner, he should sign for the money on the petty cash voucher. If you yourself take out the money for fares, for instance, then you sign the voucher. Whenever you make a purchase for the office, obtain a receipt and attach it to the voucher.

If you proceed methodically, the total cash in the box, plus the total amount shown on the vouchers, will equal the amount of the float at any time during the accounting period. At the end of the period, whether monthly, fortnightly or weekly, you enter the amounts on the petty cash slips in the petty cash book and balance it up. The amount spent is then refunded. This way of handling the petty cash is known as the Imprest System.

Practice varies from company to company as to whether expenditure is broken down and entered into various columns or simply entered without analysis. Even though your float may be small, you should take great care of the cash box; always lock it when not in use, never leaving it on the desk in your absence.

## Wages and salaries

In a small company one person is usually responsible for calculating and paying wages and salaries. In larger organisations there is a wages section within the accounting department.

*Wages* usually refers to the remuneration of workers who are paid weekly, whereas *salaries* is the term used for monthly paid staff. Wages and salaries can be paid in cash, by cheque, by credit transfer or by Giro transfer.

On pay day each employee receives a pay slip showing how the amount paid is composed. The basic composition of all wages and salaries is the same, namely:

Dr

| Receipts | Date | Details | No. | Total | Postage | Stationery | Travel | Office Ex. | VAT |
|---|---|---|---|---|---|---|---|---|---|
| £ | 198- | | | £ | | | | | |
| 40.00 | Mar.1 | Cash received | | | | | | | |
| | Mar.3 | Milk | 1 | 1.20 | | | | 1.20 | |
| | Mar.5 | Bus fare to stationer | 2 | 0.85 | | | 0.85 | | |
| | Mar.7 | Airmail envelopes | 3 | 2.20 | | 2.00 | | | 20 |
| | Mar.9 | Tea & Sugar | 4 | 1.75 | | | | 1.75 | |
| | Mar.9 | Parcel postage | 5 | 1.60 | 1.60 | | | | |
| | Mar.11 | Stamps | 6 | 4.80 | 4.80 | | | | |
| | Mar.14 | Taxi fare to printer | 7 | 1.80 | | | 1.80 | | |
| | | | | 14.20 | 6.40 | 2.00 | 2.65 | 2.95 | 20 |
| | Mar.14 | Balance | c/d | 25.80 | | | | | |
| 40.00 | | | | 40.00 | | | | | |
| 25.80 | Mar.14 | Balance | b/d | | | | | | |
| 14.20 | Mar.14 | Cash received | | | | | | | |

Fig. 12.4   A page from a petty cash book duly balanced

(*a*)   The basic rate plus overtime gives the gross wage/salary

(*b*)   The gross wage/salary plus allowances and minus deductions gives the net wage/salary

Allowances include such items as 'mileage' for employees who regularly use their own cars for business, and commission on sales.

Deductions are of two kinds:

1   *Statutory*, that is, those which must be made by law. These are (*a*) Income Tax (Pay-as-you-earn or PAYE), and (*b*) National Insurance. The National Insurance Scheme provides cash benefits for unemployment, sickness and invalidity, maternity, widowhood, retirement and death. A small portion of this contribution also goes to the National Health Service, which provides medical attention for everyone.

2   *Voluntary*, which can include contributions to a company pension scheme, company sports or social club, private health insurance scheme, trade union subscription or Save-as-You-Earn investment.

The National Insurance deductions are usually calculated by referring to contribution tables supplied by the Department of Health and Social Security. PAYE deductions are calculated by referring to the tax tables supplied to employers by the tax office to which the company is attached.

If you were responsible for working out the wages and salaries in your company, you would be well advised to visit the office of your company's Inspector of Taxes, in order to learn how to use the tax tables and which forms have to be completed for new employees, those leaving the company, temporary workers, and so on. You should also acquire a copy of *The Employer's Guide to National Insurance Contributions* and *The Employer's Guide to PAYE*, which respectively give full details of statutory deductions and how to calculate them.

## Accounting terms and records

Nothing has changed more radically in the past twenty years than the ways in which calculations are made and financial records kept in business. It was in the accounts department that the computer was first introduced, replacing not only mechanical calculations but also manual entries in record books. Book-keepers now keep books only in small organisations, and so this term is seldom heard nowadays.

So we have 'record books' which are no longer books, or not always books, and operations which are carried out only in theory, or which are still carried out only in some companies, or which are variously contrived.

Theoretically, then, daily transactions are recorded first in the appropriate book of original entry, and later transferred, or *posted*, to the ledger accounts. These books of original entry include the *cash book*, which records cash transactions; the *purchase book*, which gives details of items bought on credit; the *returns outwards book*, which lists purchases returned to the supplier for one reason or another; the *sales book*, which records items sold on credit; the *returns inwards book*, which records goods sold, but returned by customers; and the *journal*, which takes in items which do not belong in any of the books mentioned above, mainly end-of-year adjustments such as *depreciation*, which is the decrease in value of fixed assets as a result of wear and tear or accidental damage.

In addition to the books of original entry, a set of *subsidiary books* is kept. We have already mentioned two of these, the *postage book* and the *petty cash book*. Another very important one is the *wages book*, which records the wages paid, and how they were calculated.

Here are some of most common accounting terms:

*Account*   A record of transactions concerning a person, asset or activity.

Balancing an account is done by comparing the total debit entries with the total credit entries to see which is the larger. The difference is then added to the lesser side, thereby equalising the total. You have a credit balance if the credit entries are the greater, and a debit balance if the debit entries are the greater.

*Assets*   Items of value to a business, such as buildings, furniture and equipment, or money owing.

Current assets are those which are temporarily held and easily converted into cash, or cash itself, of course.

Fixed assets are long-term assets, such as plant and machinery, furniture and fittings.

*Balance sheet* A summary of the financial state of a business at the end of its financial year.

*Capital* Funds provided by the owners to run the business.

*Creditor* A person or company to whom money is owed.

*Debtor* A person or company owing money to the business.

*Goodwill* An intangible yet vital asset. It is the value of the knowhow of the business and the faith and confidence its customers have in it.

*Income and expenditure account* As the name implies, this is a record of income and expenditure. It is drawn up once a year by professional organisations, clubs and societies, and other nonprofit-making organisations.

*Ledger* A collection of accounts. It used to be a very large and heavy book, but nowadays it is more likely to be a set of cards on which entries are made by machine.

*Liability* This is the opposite to an asset, being items owed to external individuals or companies.

*Loan* Capital borrowed from a bank or other sources to finance the business.

*Profit and loss account* This is an account of the profit or loss the company has made for its financial year. The *gross profit* is the total profit before expenses are deducted and the *net profit* is the profit remaining after the various expenses are deducted from the gross profit.

*Turnover* The volume of business or net sales over a period of time, e.g. one year. It is arrived at by subtracting sales returns from total sales.

**Questions**

1   You are a secretary in a small firm and are responsible for some cash handling. Explain to your junior how to deal with the following while you are away on holiday:
    (*a*)   Remittances received in the incoming mail;
    (*b*)   Cash and cheques that she must pay into the bank;
    (*c*)   Acknowledging the receipt of (*a*) and (*b*), with guidance on when this is or is not necessary;
    (*d*)   Balancing the Petty Cash account (imprest system) and reopening it.      (LCC PSC Office Organisation and Secretarial Procedures)

2   Your employer gives you several cheques he wishes to be paid into his personal bank account, but his bank is in his home town fifty miles away. Which banking service would you use? (Pitman Secretarial Practice Intermediate)

3   Your chief has asked you to order a booklet from Her Majesty's Stationery Office. It is priced at 25p. Which method would you use to pay for it?

4   Your employer has sent a memorandum to all office staff informing them that from next month onwards salaries would be paid by credit transfer. What does this imply, and what advantages does this method of payment have for you and for your employer?

5   Many importers of British goods abroad pay for the goods by Letter of Credit. How does this work?

6   What is a crossed cheque?

7   In view of the increase in the amount of work you handle, Mr Watson (Your chief) has suggested that the Works Manager's secretary, Janet Curtis, might take over from you the responsibility for the office cash. Using the documents on p. 172 and 174 as guidance, state the purpose of each and the procedure to be followed in obtaining and handling office cash.      (RSA Secretarial Duties Stage II)

8   (*a*)   Describe and explain the purpose of a Bank Statement.
    (*b*)   Why might you draw up a Bank Reconciliation Statement? Mention 5 types of entry that might be included in it. (LCCI PSC Office Organisation and Secretarial Procedures)

# 13

# Reprography

Reprography is a fairly new word in the English language, meaning any method of reproducing a document. The first and most obvious way of doing this is to use carbon paper, and we saw in Chapter 6 how you can obtain up to fifteen copies with supermanifold carbon paper. If you use carbonless paper, usually known as NCR (no carbon required), you can obtain up to seven copies on a manual typewriter, and up to nine copies on an electric typewriter. These are obviously the methods you must use if you simply need a few copies of a letter or document which you are typing.

If the company you work for has an electronic memory typewriter or a word processor, duplicating documents will be even easier. With an electronic memory typewriter, a letter can be automatically stored away and then retrieved and printed at the touch of a button. Alternatively, individual sentences can be stored, to be retrieved later, amended, incorporated with new material, and reproduced automatically. If the word processor has an appropriate print attachment, any number of copies can be printed automatically at the touch of a button. More information on these electronic machines is given in the next chapter.

When we come to actual duplicating, photocopying and printing equipment, we are not talking about three absolutely distinct and separate types of machinery. On the contrary, there are many machines which work in a different way giving practically identical results. Manufacturers sometimes confuse the issue still further by their choice of name. For instance, some manufacturers refer to their products as 'copier-duplicators', and at least one company calls its electronic typewriter a 'personal electronic printer'. It is none the less a fact that these machines work differently, and on this basis we can single out the following four methods of reproduction: spirit duplicating, ink duplicating, offset-lithography and photo-copying.

## Spirit duplicating

This method is also known as *hectograph* duplicating. First of all a master has to be produced, which can be handwritten, drawn or typewritten on a special paper called a *spirit master*. A specially coated transfer sheet called *hectograph carbon* is placed behind the master, carbon side facing the back of the master, and finally a backing sheet is inserted. Transfer sheets are available in a number of colours, so if you want to use another colour, you simply remove the transfer sheet and put in the required colour.

Corrections are made either by painting over the error with a correcting fluid or by scraping off the error with a special knife or razor blade. When the incorrect impression has been treated, a slip of new carbon must be inserted behind the master before typing over, since the dye will have been removed from the original carbon. The transfer sheet can be used only once and must therefore be discarded once the master has been typed. Unused strips can, however, usefully be retained for correction purposes.

When the master is completed, it is fixed to the spirit duplicating machine, reverse side upwards, that is, the side that has been in contact with the transfer sheet will face you as you operate the machine. You then feed through your copy paper and receive your finished copies on the opposite side of the machine. No ink is involved except the dye in the transfer sheet, which is gently released as the copy paper, moistened with spirit, is pressed against it. This means that spirit duplicating is quite a clean process, although some of the dye may end up on your hands. It is easily washed off.

At least sixty good copies can be obtained from one master, and sometimes many more, but this depends both on the skill with which the master has been prepared, and the careful use of the duplicator, with just enough but not too much spirit being used. The master can be stored for further use by carefully removing it from the duplicator, backing it with a flimsy sheet of paper and keeping it in a safe place where no pressure will be put on it.

Spirit duplicating is sometimes used for producing sets of documents from a single master, such as invoices or coloured diagrams. It can also be used for internal memoranda, but is not otherwise suitable for use outside the company.

## Ink duplicating

This method is also known as *stencil* duplicating, as a stencil is used as the master. The stencil consists of a waxed sheet, a thin carbon, and a backing sheet, all held together by the stencil head, which is perforated so that it can be fixed onto the machine. Sometimes the carbon is not included in the set, in which case it should be added, face upwards, between the wax sheet and the backing sheet. If a copy is required on the backing sheet, then another carbon must be inserted under the first one, this time facing the backing sheet. The stencil is then inserted into the typewriter and the document typed, taking care to disengage the ribbon first.

Corrections can be made in two ways: first by 'painting' the error over with correcting fluid, and secondly by patching. If you want to correct a small error, first run a fingernail gently over the error to smooth out the fibres of the sheet, then separate it from the carbon by inserting a pencil behind. Next, carefully apply correcting fluid over the error. Allow it to dry, take out the pencil, and type over.

If the error is a large one and you need to replace a whole paragraph, cut out the offending paragraph, type out the fresh paragraph on a clean stencil, cut it out so that it overlaps a little and 'paint' it into place on the original stencil with your correcting fluid. It is advisable to 'paint' both sides of the stencil. This method is known as *grafting*.

Stencils may also be cut by machine. Roneo Alcatel, a leading manufacturer of this type of equipment, offers an electronic stencil cutter which is suitable for line drawing as well as typewritten work, and another model which is suitable for full colour work. Both of these machines also produce plates for offset printing work, which will be dealt with later in this chapter. These scanners, as they are also called, are very simple to use: the virgin stencil and the material to be copied are clipped side by side onto the roller, the machine is set and your stencil is cut for you in a matter of minutes.

There are two main types of ink duplicating machine, but both are operated in the same way. Read the maker's instructions carefully before you begin, and work methodically without rushing, as running off stencils requires care. Fix the stencil head to the machine carefully and lay the stencil smoothly over the drum, so that it does not crease. Multi-colour work is quite simple to do on the modern machines. Inks are available in fourteen colours. To change colour, simply remove one cylinder and replace it with another.

It is possible to obtain as many as six thousand copies from a single stencil if it has been well cut, carefully handled and properly stored. Before storage, lay it flat on a table, inky surface upwards, press gently with a sheet of blotting paper to remove the surplus ink, and then store flat in a labelled file or secured with a bulldog clip and threaded on a rail. Make sure that no weights are placed on stencils which are stored flat, otherwise they will be ruined.

Paper of various qualities and sizes can be used, including 3 in × 5 in (7.5 cm × 12.5 cm) cards. Results can look quite professional, so this method is suitable for producing reports, parts lists and even internal newsletters.

## Offset-lithography

The master used for offset-lithography is sometimes, but not always, called a plate. A master can quite simply be typed on an electric typewriter with a carbon ribbon or it can be produced by a word processing machine, by high-speed computer or by an Offset Mastermaker. As we saw, some stencil cutters also produce masters for offset lithography, while the Roneo Alcatel Electrostatic Offset Mastermaker is specially designed for offset work. Offset plates can also be made of metal, which, of course, makes them much more durable. Typewritten plates can, obviously, be corrected in the usual way and can be stored and re-used, but once again care must be taken not to put pressure on them during storage.

The modern offset duplicator is small, compact, quiet, largely automatic and extremely simple to operate. It is just a question of attaching your master, selecting the number of copies you need,

**Fig. 13.1** A stencil cutter and platemaker for offset printing (Roneoscan)

placing your paper in the feed tray, and manipulating the control knob.

Full colour is of course possible with these machines and results are not *like* printing, but actually *are* printing, since this is a printing process brought into the office. Producing full colour work is a little more complex, of course, but it is not a task often expected of a secretary.

Many companies produce their own advertising material, letter-heads and forms on these machines, which are suitable for any type of work requiring a long run.

## Photocopying

The plain paper copier (PPC) is by far the most widely used copying system available today. With these copiers it is no longer a question of producing a master and then duplicating it, but rather of obtaining one or more copies from an original. Fig. 13.2 shows a plain paper copier which can be fitted with an optional document feeder and automatic collator.

**Fig. 13.2**   A plain paper copier (Mita)

More and more of these copiers are coming on to the market al
the time and they vary in size from desk copiers smaller than ;
typewriter to large models more suitable for the print-room. Specia
features which were once to be found only in large machines ar
frequently available even in the smallest models.

Plain paper copiers can produce between six and thirty copies
minute, depending on the model and make; some of them ca
accept any size of paper, from A5 to A3 or B4; many of them ca
reproduce from single sheets, book pages and even three
dimensional items, while others can even reproduce compute
print-outs and transparencies. The smallest machine can reproduc
between one and ten copies, while the largest can be set to repr
duce up to ninety-nine copies. Most machines need up to fou
minutes' warm-up time, but others need no warm-up time at all; th
first copy is produced in four to eight seconds, according to mak
and model.

Some copiers reduce documents to a more manageable size an
others can both reduce and enlarge. Quite a number of machine
have a so-called run/interrupt feature. This means that if you hav

just set the machine to run off ninety copies, and you suddenly need to break off to do something very urgent, you can just stop the machine at the touch of a button, then restart it later and it will pick up the job where it left off. A few machines automatically collate the copies as they are produced, and some machines automatically print on both sides of the paper.

These machines are simplicity itself to operate. You simply lift the flap or cover, place the document face down on the machine, pull the cover down over it, select the number of copies you need either by turning the dial or pressing the appropriate buttons, and start the machine. There are variations, of course, according to the make. Some machines have a micro-computer touch sensor control panel in which case you just touch the appropriate numbers on the panel to get the number of copies you want. On some models the paper is supplied in cassettes containing two hundred and fifty sheets. The cassette is loaded into the machine and the sheets are automatically fed in as required.

Minolta make a copier which produces copies in blue or red, as well as black, but full colour copiers for the office are not yet available. You can, however, get copies in full colour by using a colour copying service, such as Chromacopy, which has agencies all over the world.

Technically, not all copiers use the same process, but they all give the same excellent results and all are easy and clean to operate, so there is no need to go into technicalities. Only recently, both wet and dry copiers existed, but the 'wets' have been outclassed and the dry copier, micro-computer controlled, is beginning to dominate the market.

## Selecting a machine

There could be no question of your being asked to decide single-handed on the purchase of a machine costing a few thousand pounds, but your opinion might well be sought on a possible purchase.

The first question to ask yourself in such a case is: what type of work is the machine needed for? If you need to copy original documents, some of them coming from outside the office, then obviously you need a photocopier. All you need do is decide on the size of machine you need. Arm yourself with as many leaflets as you can get hold of, and see how the various models compare, not forgetting to consider price.

If you need to duplicate work originating in the office, then you need to consider the length of run most frequently required, and the quality of reproduction needed. If long runs of first-class printed material are frequently needed, then an offset duplicator would be suitable.

Another point to consider is what other equipment is already available in the office, so that the new purchase augments the present facilities, but does not duplicate them.

**Questions**

1   Describe the most effective method which could be used to deal with FOUR of the following tasks:
    (a)   producing twelve copies (one for each director) of a first draft of the Chairman's report to the shareholders
    (b)   producing an offset master of material containing some mathematical and scientific symbols
    (c)   producing a leaflet, the text of which must have justified right-hand margins
    (d)   typing a report with eight copies in a foreign language
    (e)   dealing with a heavy bulk of correspondence which requires standardised paragraphs plus some individual (personalised) information
    (f)   sending the same letter to all your customers, advising them of changes in your cash and quantity discounts.    (LCC PSC Office Organisation and Secretarial Procedures)

2   Describe a variety of methods and equipment which might be used to reduce to a minimum the time spent on addressing envelopes.    (LCC PSC Office Organisation and Secretarial Procedure)

3   Your employer has asked for your opinion in helping to select a suitable copying machine for the office. What preparatory work would you do, and which questions would you ask yourself before writing a memorandum with your recommendations?

# 14

# Office Equipment

The electronic office is no longer the office of tomorrow: it is the office of today. Any company which has a mind to can go out now and equip itself with an electronic office and furthermore, there is a choice from a number of systems. But what *is* an electronic office, anyway?

First of all, a better name for it would be 'computer-based office'. It is an office equipped with word processors and microcomputers; picture transmission equipment, that is, facsimile machines and viewdata; telephone and dictation equipment – all linked together and fully integrated. Some people call it the Interactive Office.

All of the systems on the market are necessarily similar, although each claims to be more complete than the others. The Sperrylink System, for instance, includes word processing, electronic mail, electronic filing and retrieving, an electronic phone book, message-taker and diary, calculator, personal computer, and access to computers outside the company. All of these facilities are linked together in a network of desk stations, where the basic functions of typing reports, filing and retrieving information, and so on are carried out.

The Plessey System, called IBIS (Internal Business Information System), is linked together by its private digital exchange (PDX), which is able to transmit voice, text and data, unlike the ordinary telephone which transmits voice alone. The heart of IBIS is a piece of equipment called the Plessey Dataplug. It looks rather like a desk telephone and its function is to give non-Plessey work stations access to the IBIS network.

**Fig. 14.1**  The electronic office, as seen by Sperry Univac

This brings us to the colossal problem now facing manufacturers and users of electronic equipment, namely that many of these machines – microcomputers, word processors, etc. – are unable to communicate with each other or with existing mainframe computer systems, because they are incompatible. So the Sperrylink electronic mail system, for instance, enables letters and memoranda to be sent electronically to any of the company's branches, anywhere in the world, but not necessarily to another company just down the road. Exactly the same problem was described in Chapter 4 when we learned that British Telecom's electronic mail service enables mail to be transmitted electronically in seconds to another desk within a company, but not outside the company. We saw this difficulty again in Chapter 5 when considering the incompatibility of some of the Fax machines.

The Plessey Dataplug helps alleviate this problem and so does ITT's information transfer module, but the problem of incompatibility of equipment is still a major stumbling block.

Another point to bear in mind is that by no means all companies are rushing to automate. For instance, a 1982 survey revealed that the UK editorial offices of newspaper, magazine and book publishers – which one might expect to be in the forefront of information and communications technology – had hardly been touched by the electronic revolution: fewer than one in six of such offices had anything more advanced than a conventional typewriter. So it is not impossible that your first job may involve wielding a manual typewriter.

## Typewriters

The typewriter first came on the scene in 1874 and remained virtually unchanged until the advent of the electric models in the 1920s. However, as we have seen, the manual typewriter is still with us and in use in many offices. The electric typewriter is, of course, easier on the arm muscles, produces clearer copy, and considerably increases the speed at which material can be typed. When proportional spacing was introduced in 1944 the appearance of the typewritten page improved even further, as a typed letter could then look almost like printing.

The next major breakthrough was the introduction of the IBM Selectric typewriter in 1961. It came to be nicknamed the 'golfball' typewriter because of the spherical printing element it uses in place of typebars. These 'golfballs' are available in a number of different typefaces, including Orator, an extra large and clear typeface suitable for typing speeches, and OCR (Optical Character Recognition), which is a typeface computers can 'read' if the text is fed through an OCR device.

The latest model Selectric has a number of other interesting innovations, the best of all from the typist's point of view being the self-correcting device. If you strike the wrong key, you just press the correcting key, re-type the error to obliterate it, or as the manufacturer says, to 'lift it off the page', and then type in the correct letters. Another feature is the option of typing ten or twelve characters to the inch. This is known as *pitch* – 12 pitch is recommended for forms and long texts, and 10 for correspondence. Just a flick of the switch and you can select the pitch you want. Another option is coloured ribbons, with a choice of blue, brown or green.

The next step is the electronic typewriter. Depending on make and model, electronic typewriters offer automatic margin setting, carriage return, underlining, double spacing, bold printing, and tabulation. Ribbon changing is greatly simplified by the use of a cassette system and error correction is automatic.

In most electronic typewriters a typewheel, often called a daisy-wheel, replaces the old typebars, except the IBM which uses the familiar golfball. All machines offer a choice of pitch. Almost all electronic typewriters have a 'memory' – that is, the capacity to retain material that has been typed and recall it as required. Memory capacity can vary from 185 characters in one model to 16 000 characters, equal to eight full pages, in another. Even with a memory of only a few hundred characters you can recall such repetitive items as the date, reference and salutation and insert them as required at the touch of a button.

There are also electronic typewriters which incorporate a calculator enabling the operator to do figure work, prepare invoices and produce daily statistics, listings and tables. Some electronic typewriters even have a display panel so you can see what you are typing before it is committed to paper.

## Word processors

With word processing we enter the realms of computer technology. Word processing is, in fact, the application of computer technology to the production of typed documents. Material is not typed directly onto paper, as occurs with a conventional typewriter, but appears on a Visual Display Unit (VDU). When the operator has read the text on display and is satisfied that it is correct, she touches the 'Print' button and the printed page is produced. The printer is usually an independent peripheral of the word processing system.

All the refinements included in the electronic typewriter are also offered by the word processor: there is a choice of pitch, automatic margin setting, underlining, carriage return, double spacing, bold printing, and tabulation. Error correction is automatic.

Word processors have a bigger 'memory' than electronic typewriters, and can store material on disc, card or tape. Such material can be retrieved for modification or amplification with or without the production of an intermediate typed draft.

Some word processors even permit the operator to check spellings. The IBM Display System, for instance, has a dictionary of 50 000 commonly used words stored on a diskette. The operator can summon this service and check the copy against the dictionary.

The final document is usually produced under computer control on a high-quality printer. The appearance is that of high quality electric typewriting. There is a choice of printers on the market, including one which automatically prints virtually any number of copies of a document at the touch of a button.

These are the main applications of the word processor:

1 *The production of standard letters*, such as mailing 'shots', which can be personalised by making insertions in the body of the letter and are addressed by the touch of a button from stored addresses.
2 *Text editing*. All you have to do is 'key in' the new sentence or phrase and, when given the correct command, the machine will insert it in the right place and readjust the remaining text. Typing and retyping of drafts becomes a thing of the past. This facility is ideal for all documents requiring various amendments, such as reports, minutes of meetings or contracts.
3 *Storage of standard paragraphs or clauses* for inclusion in standard letters, legal documents or insurance policies.
4 *Form design*. Forms can be stored in the memory and variable details filled in automatically by merging two files.
5 *Label and envelope addressing* and matching-in addresses to letters.
6 *Updating price lists* (if the machine incorporates a calculator).

There are said to be over one thousand different word processors on the market and it is as well to bear in mind that not all of them have the same functions. Even the large VDU is not common to all word processors. Some have panels displaying one or two lines at a time.

In a great many offices the word processor is used quite simply as a glorified typewriter, but in reality it can be very much more, as we saw at the beginning of this chapter. It can be the centrepiece of the electronic office, handling photo-typesetting, sending and receiving electronic mail, accessing public or private Viewdata, sending and receiving Telex messages, sorting, retrieving and filing information,

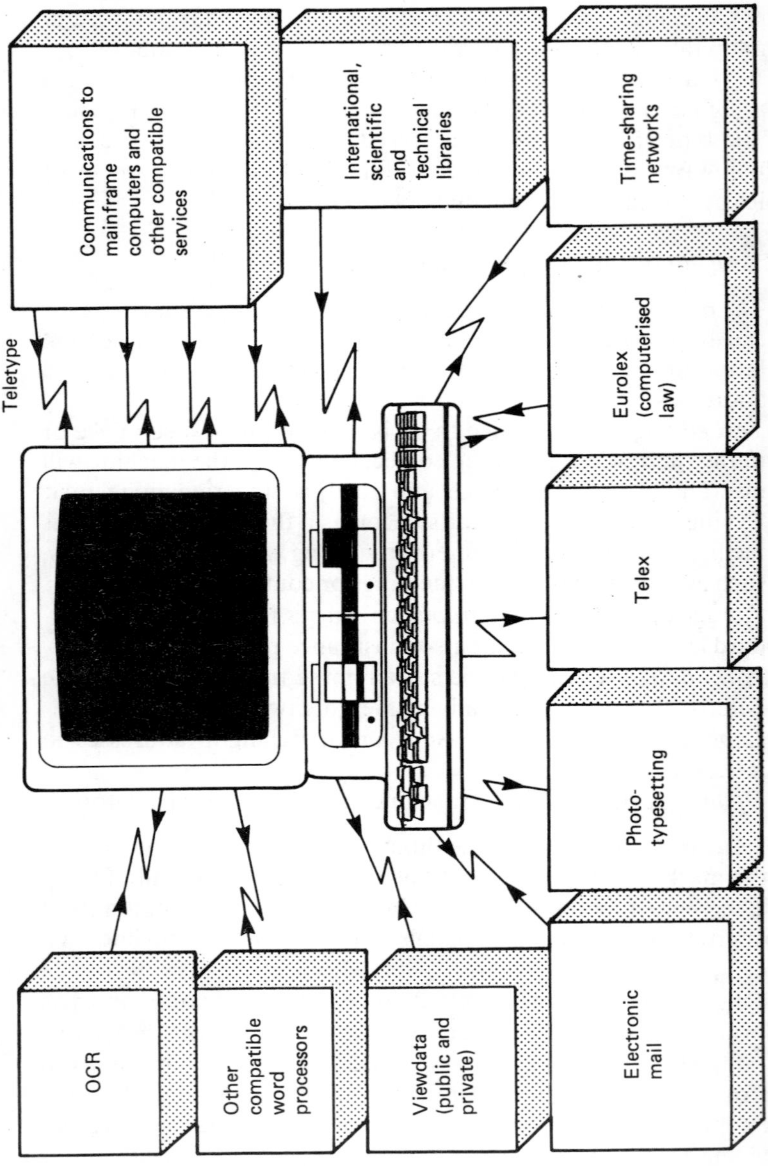

**Fig. 14.2** Word processor applications (Wordplex)

Communications to mainframe computers and other compatible services

International, scientific and technical libraries

Time-sharing networks

Teletype

Eurolex (computerised law)

Telex

Photo-typesetting

OCR

Other compatible word processors

Viewdata (public and private)

Electronic mail

storing and printing the information gleaned and even more. For instance, the Wordplex 80-4 calls itself two systems in one and is able to carry out two operations simultaneously.

## Dictating and transcription equipment

While some of the old dictating equipment, recording on disc, is still in use, the market is now dominated by the tape recorder. The cassettes housing the tape are available in three sizes: Compact (also known as the standard C-type), the Mini and the Micro, which is a minute box only one-third the size of the standard cassette. All sizes have recording time ranging between thirty minutes and two hours, according to make and type. Grundig have their own cassette called the Stenocassette 30. The tape is one-sided, extra thick and runs for thirty minutes.

The trend to miniaturisation extends all the way from the micro-cassette to the portable dictator which you could lose in your hand and transcribers much smaller than portable typewriters.

The latest transcription equipment has all the advantages of microprocessor technology, with sensor panel control, visual displays showing where the letters begin and end, and an alphanumeric readout giving the length of the next letter in minutes and seconds.

Some machines serve both as dictating and transcribing equipment. When dictation is finished, the secretary takes the machine away, plugs in the headset and foot pedal and begins transcribing. There is even a machine which combines portable dictator, desktop dictator and transcriber.

Portable dictators are very popular: engineers and surveyors use them on site, salesmen take them on the road, and executives take them along when they travel. The result is that a secretary is likely to have a number of tapes coming in for transcription.

It is also possible to dictate from an ordinary telephone or from an internal telephone network. The dictator is linked directly to a transcribing machine on the typist's desk. There are two machines, so that one can receive dictation while the other is being used for transcription.

The next step is centralised dictation. The dictator is linked not to a secretary's desk, but to a dictation centre, where a number of typists are ready to transcribe and a supervisor takes charge of the 'traffic'. When the dictator has finished, he or she replaces the receiver. This automatically stops the tape, ejects the cassette, and sends it on its way either to the top of an output stack or into a carousel, depending on which system is used. The supervisor then hands out the tapes to be transcribed. Some of these systems are highly computerised and can be used in conjunction with word processors and teleprinters, as well as ordinary typewriters. There are also simpler less sophisticated systems.

## Addressing machines

The most up-to-date way of addressing large mailings is by computer. Over half of the big publishing companies and direct-mail businesses use this method. There are a number of computerised addressing systems on the market to be used in conjunction with a word processor. They enable addresses to be printed on self-adhesive labels, continuous stationery or direct onto envelopes. The addresses are stored on floppy discs for re-use as required.

The older methods involve the creation of a master, which is then fed into a machine for printing. Masters can be embossed on metal or plastic cards or simply typed on metal foil plates. Alternatively, stencil masters can be cut on a typewriter, using special cards surrounded by a frame. Another alternative is the spirit master. In the Addressograph Farringdon system, addresses are typed on a master patch label which is then detached from the hectograph carbon backed sheet and attached to a master address card. There are even simpler systems: the addresses are typed on the specially-treated portion of an address card, which then becomes both master and file card. Selective mailing is taken care of quite simply by marking the cards with a felt-tipped pen in the appropriate positions. In addition, the cards are colour-coded for easy classification.

The addressing machines themselves are available in a very broad range to suit the smallest company with a mailing list of a hundred addresses, and the giant with a mailing list of over half a million names. The small machines are hand-operated. You just stack the master cards in the hopper, feed in the envelopes and turn the handle. At the other end of the scale are the automatic machines capable of turning out seven thousand or more addressed items an hour. If you use a special attachment the machine will even select electronically those addresses you want to use.

## Teleprinters

The electronic age has caught up with teleprinters too and, as a result, the new generation teleprinters are called Telex terminals. The first two, called Puma and Cheetah, were launched by British Telecom. Puma looks exactly like a typewriter with a handful of extra keys. It can store messages for later transmission, as well as incoming messages; make calls and transmit messages automatically, while the machine is unattended; keep trying to get through if a terminal is busy; be programmed to remember up to twenty-five frequently used numbers and call them automatically in response to a two-character code and permits operators to correct the messages in store, as well as to make inserts or deletions and to rearrange the text to avoid split words or unsightly gaps.

Cheetah looks more like a word processor, with a full-sized visual display unit (VDU). It offers most of the same facilities as Puma, with a few added advantages. Like other word processors, it enables the text to be edited at will. Messages are typed directly into the Cheetah electronic memory and can be retrieved for transmittal or editing at the touch of a key.

As we saw earlier, British Telecom no longer has a monopoly in the telecommunications field and consequently other companies are busy bringing out their own teleprinters. One of these is called Transtel and is very much like Cheetah. There are others, with more on the way, no doubt.

Meanwhile, not every company has the most up-to-date electronic teleprinter: there are semi-electronic models and the standard machines are still in use. They work rather like an electric typewriter. Most of them have a punched tape attachment, which enables a 'dry run' to be made with the teleprinter switched to 'local'. While the message is being typed, it is punched into a paper tape at the same time. The message can then be corrected if necessary. Then the tape is fitted to the machine, the teleprinter is connected to the subscriber at the other end, and the message is sent automatically from the tape at twice the normal speed of the operator. This is a very useful device when difficult messages have

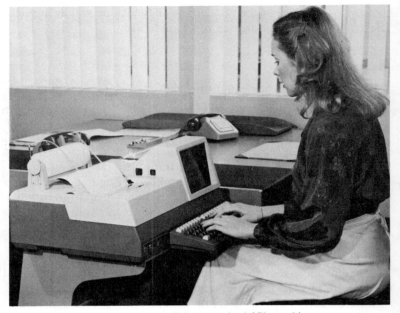

**Fig. 14.3** A Telex terminal (Cheetah)

to be put through. In addition, it leaves the teleprinter free to receive incoming messages and it also saves money, since sending Telex messages is far from cheap. The use of tape is, of course, no longer necessary with electronic teleprinters, as messages can be edited before transmission, as we have seen.

The Telex is, of course, a public service. It is also possible for a company to have its own private teleprinter service linked by its own circuit, or it can be part of an integrated office system.

## Calculators

Nowadays almost every company employee, from clerk to managing director, has a pocket calculator within easy reach, which is used to carry out any type of calculation required during the course of the day's work.

Calculators do have many more complex uses, however. The more advanced versions are desktop models with print and display facilities. They can print only, display only, or do both. They can add, subtract, multiply and divide, and work out percentages, interest and exchange rates – all within seconds. There are also calculators which carry out far more complex calculations, such as compound interest and bond yields, and others which handle sums involving time. They can be used for calculating and checking payroll totals, invoice extensions, foreign exchange rates, and so on.

Some calculators can be fitted with a special OCR font, so that the print-out can be read by a computer. Print-outs are otherwise used to provide printed proof of the accuracy of the calculations and for attaching to documents for future reference and checking.

We have already seen how many electronic typewriters incorporate calculating facilities. There are also combination machines, such as the Facit Electronic Typewriter/Invoicing machine, which has a full-scale calculator built into the keyboard, with its own display panel. Calculators can also be powered by electricity or battery, and there are even some models powered by solar cells.

# Computers

To paraphrase a British Standards 3527:1962 definition, a computer is a machine which can perform numerous arithmetical and logical operations without intervention by a human operator during a run. The items of information, known as data, first have to be fed to the computer by means of an input peripheral. The computer is then instructed on what to do with this data. These instructions are known as a *program* (not *programme* in computer parlance). Finally the processed material is extracted from the computer via output peripherals.

### Input peripherals

Information can be fed into a computer in a number of ways, sometimes directly and sometimes via a converter device known as a reader. There are, for instance, Magnetic Ink Character Readers (MICR) which 'read' the type of magnetic ink characters printed on cheques; Optical Character Readers (OCR), which 'read' the OCR typeface available on some typewriters and word processors; document readers which 'read' documents produced on typewriters, printers, cash registers, and so on; and electronic micropads on which information is written and read by a sensing device and conveyed to the computer. Other input peripherals are punched cards, paper tapes, keyboards and visual display units.

**Output peripherals**
There is a variety of these too: printers, which produce the required information on paper; visual display units, graph plotters, microfilm, magnetic tape or disc.

**The Central Processing Unit**
The unit which processes the information is known as the Central Processing Unit (CPU), also known as *hardware*. It consists of three parts: the calculating unit, the 'memory' where the information is stored, and the control unit, which 'supervises' the carrying out of the program.

**Software**
The computer cannot, of course, work on its own. A 'program', or set of step-by-step instructions, has to be worked out for it. Neither does the computer understand English, so programs have to written out in one of a number of computer 'languages'. A computer language frequently used in business is COBOL (COmmon Business Oriented Language). These computer programs are known as *software*.

Computers are not really new. They have been with us since the early 1940s and were used in business first of all in accounts departments. At first computers were huge machines needing a whole room, complete with reinforced floor, to house them, and their cost was astronomical. Now there are desktop models selling at a price that individuals can afford.

This revolution has been brought about by the advent of the silicon chip. Circuits are printed, layer upon layer, on a tiny piece of silicon. The result is a microprocessor which enables machines to carry out the functions previously performed by large and expensive mainframe installations.

Some businesses, such as banks, are almost completely computerised. Other large companies computerise wages, salaries and pensions, production control, ledger accounts and credit control, stock ordering and stock control. Some medium-sized and even small businesses are also attracted by computerisation. Indeed, many desktop computers are especially designed for the small company. They can deal with all the operations already mentioned and perform as a word processor as well.

We have already mentioned many computer applications in this book: the word processor, viewdata, electronic mailing, Telex terminals, and indeed the integrated office systems, which one might describe as the apotheosis of the computer.

Properly handled, computerisation can bring speed and efficiency to a business to a degree never before envisaged, let alone achieved, but it is wise not to get too carried away by it and to consider all other options.

**Questions**
1 Give three examples of electronic equipment using a visual display unit (VDU). (Pitman Secretarial Practice Intermediate)
2 You use an electric typewriter. What action affecting the typewriter must you take before leaving the office at night? (Pitman Secretarial Practice Intermediate)
3 Once the conventional typewriter keyboard has been mastered and proficiency obtained, it is possible to train a typist to operate a number of modern business machines successfully. Describe three such machines, and explain clearly their purpose in office work. (LCC PSC Office Organisation and Secretarial Procedures)
4 Describe four operations which a word processor can carry out.
5 What do you understand by centralised dictation? How does this work?
6 Give a brief description of (*a*) software, and (*b*) hardware.
7 List three ways in which a computer can be used in an office.

# 15

# Personnel

## Recruitment

When an employer needs to recruit staff, several avenues are open to him. In practice, however, he tends to use one or two sources only. The sources of manpower that could be tapped include the following:

1 *The company's present employees* This is where all recruitment campaigns should begin, as it offers the company's employees the opportunity to try for promotion, or simply to broaden their experience by moving into another department. Vacancies can be posted on the bulletin board and employees invited to apply for them or to recommend a friend.

2 *Chance applicants* When people make speculative applications for work, their names, addresses and details of the work they are seeking should be kept on record. Such people have shown some initiative, and have often done some research into the company and are keen to work for it.

3 *Trade, industrial and professional associations* These are an excellent source of applicants. Many associations have their own magazine, news-sheet, circular or bulletin board, in which vacancies can be listed, and some of them have a placement officer who is eager to help.

4 *Schools and colleges* These are a rich source of applicants.

5 *Labour unions* In some industries the unions supply employers with workers or at least a list of available members.

6 *Government Job Centres and private employment agencies*. Both

of these sources are frequently used, and many employers look no further afield.

7 *Professional selectors and searchers*  These two methods differ in that the 'Personnel Selectors' screen applicants who apply of their own free will, while 'Executive Searchers' actually go out and look for suitable employees, often attracting people away from a job by offering the temptation of a more lucrative job or an interesting opportunity. These methods are frequently used by large companies seeking scientific, technical or managerial talent.

8 *Advertising in the national, local and trade press*  This is probably the most fruitful and most commonly used recruitment method. The advertisement can either be 'open', giving the name and address of the company, or 'blind', with a box number. An 'open' advertisement usually yields more applicants, as some potential employees do not like replying to a 'mystery ad'. A 'blind ad', on the other hand, enables a company to maintain complete secrecy about its recruitment operation.

9 *Advertising on Prestel*  This is a rapidly developing way to advertise for staff.

In a medium-sized or large company, staff recruitment is carried out by the Personnel Department. In small companies, someone, perhaps the company secretary, is given the personnel function as part of his job, or the owner, one of the partners, or the managing director may take care of it.

Before recruitment begins, however, a *job description* and a *job specification* should be drawn up. The first is simply a description of the job to be done, as the name implies. The job specification, on the other hand, is a list of the attributes needed to carry out the job. For a secretary they may include typing and shorthand speeds, familiarity with various pieces of office equipment, a pleasant personality, organising ability, and so on.

## Applying for a job

If you read through the nine sources of manpower listed above, you will realise right away that some of them represent good hunting grounds for the job-seeker. In today's market if you are looking for a job, whether a first job or a greater challenge, you would be well advised to tap as many sources as you can.

It is an excellent plan to study the companies in your town or in nearby towns, and then to write and ask if they have any vacancies. In other words, try your luck as a 'chance applicant', as described in (2). However, do your homework before applying. Study one or more of the directories in your local library, for example *Kompass* and *Kelly's*, and also ask to see the annual reports of the companies you have chosen. Then find out the name of the Personnel Manager either from the directory or simply by phoning up. Read up your subject thoroughly and then send off a letter somewhat like the one shown in Fig. 15.1.

Making a speculative application has the advantage that yours could well be the only letter of that type which arrives on the Personnel Manager's desk that morning, whereas if he has placed an advertisement he can expect fifty, sixty, or even eighty or more replies. The disadvantage of writing a 'chance' letter is, of course, that there may well be no suitable vacancy.

If you are applying for an advertised job, it is a good idea to send *curriculum vitae*, accompanied by a lively, spirited letter. There are bound to be several applicants with similar qualifications for the job, so you have to do something to make yourself stand out in the crowd.

Your CV could be laid out as shown in Fig. 15.2.

If you apply 'cold' you may get a reply asking you to go in for interview. If you reply to an advertisement you are more likely to be sent an application form, as companies do not usually interview every applicant for a job. They send applicants a form to fill in, and after studying all the forms received, they draw up a so-called 'short-list'. Those candidates are interviewed and the final choice made from that group.

## Interviews

If asked to attend an interview, go along, suitably dressed and groomed, and make sure you arrive a little before the appointed time so that you are not flustered. Try to look calm and poised. Smile, and sit down when invited to do so.

If the interview you are attending is for a specific job, then you

Mr William J. Bloggs
Personnel Manager
XYZ Electronics Plc
Western Avenue
Sometown
SL8 7TY

6 June 198-

Dear Mr Bloggs

Do you need any lively, hard-working, enthusiastic
young people on your secretarial staff?

I am just about to complete a secretarial course at
the Leicestershire College of Art and Technology,
and am anxious to begin my career with a forward-
looking company which appreciates ambitious, hard-
working people who are eager to make a real contribution.

I believe that XYZ is just such a company.    I am
aware that the company has won Queen's Awards for
both export and technology, and that it has made
many acquisitions, both in Britain and overseas.

XYZ is the type of company I should like to work for.
I realise that at the moment I have only youth,
enthusiasm and energy to contribute, but I would
like to be offered an opportunity to grow with the
company and become a valuable member of the team.

My shorthand and typing speeds are respectively 100
and 50 words a minute, and while at college I
acquired basic familiarity with word processors, as
well as various other office machines including ...

I shall soon be sitting for the following public
examinations ...    In addition, while at school I
obtained external certificates in the following
academic subjects ...

I hope you will offer me an opportunity of coming in
to meet you, and look forward to hearing from you.

Yours sincerely,

**Fig. 15.1**    A sample job application letter

```
Curriculum Vitae

Name:               Angela Metcalfe

Address:            15 Willow Road.
                    Loughborough
                    Leicestershire LE12 5TW

                    Telephone:  0509 889931

Nationality:        British

Date of birth:      1 June 196-        Age now:  —

Education:          197- to 198- Loughborough High
                                 School

                    198- to 198- Leicestershire
                                 College of Art and
                                 Technology

Qualifications:     GCE O levels

                    English   B   Art     B
                    Maths     C   French B
                    Biology   C

                    To be taken: LCC Private
                                 Secretary's
                                 Certificate

                    Speeds:   Shorthand 100 wpm
                              Typing       50 wpm

Work experience:    Summer vacation jobs with Midland
                    Bank, 198- and 198-

Hobbies and
  interests:        Reading, cooking, horse-riding
                    and swimming
```

**Fig. 15.2** A sample curriculum vitae

interviewer might well begin by telling you about the job. Look him full in the face and listen intelligently. Then your interviewer will want to hear something from you, and will probably begin by going over your background, taking up the points on your application form.

This is where you must begin to unfold and let your personality come to the surface. So don't just sit there answering 'Yes', 'No', and 'That's right'. Try to enlarge on the subject. You will be asked about your hobbies, likes and dislikes, and other things not connected with work. Try to answer honestly and with some animation, but do bear in mind how what you are saying will sound at the other side of the desk. For instance, if you chat away enthusiastically about a dozen hobbies, your interviewer may well wonder whether you will have any energy and enthusiasm left for work. So be wise and admit to a few interests, otherwise you would be thought dull, but not too many! The same policy applies to everything else about yourself. Try to present the right image of yourself, in other words the image of the potentially expert secretary.

Your next trial will be the typing and shorthand test. Most typists, shorthand-typists and secretaries who are interviewed for a job are given these tests, so you must be prepared for them. Interviewers are well aware that applicants are nervous at taking a test and so usually make allowances for nerves. If you are one of those shorthand writers who feel they simply cannot make any headway without their favourite type of pen or pencil, you should take the precaution of bringing your favourite implements with you. Word processing skills are now in demand and you might be asked to work with an operator for half an hour to test your aptitude in working with machines. Whatever the situation, just do your best.

## On the job

Let us assume now that you are well qualified, presented yourself well at the interview, took the tests in your stride and have obtained the job. What then? On your first day your employer should do all he can to make you feel at home. You should be acquainted with all the mundane details, such as canteen facilities (if any), refreshment dispensers, rest-room and so on. The details of your conditions of employment should be explained to you, including holiday entitlement, sick leave and other forms of leave, hours of work, how the flexitime scheme works, if appropriate, and so on. The law stipulates that these conditions should be set down in writing within thirteen weeks of starting full-time work, but in the meantime it is useful to run through them orally. Many companies present new employees with little booklets welcoming them and giving the company history, its aims and policies.

You should then be introduced to your immediate colleagues and to those in other departments with whom you will come in contact. A general tour of the whole organisation is also very useful and enables a new employee to understand how his or her particular job fits in the organisation as a whole. Finally an employer should make sure that a new employee really knows how to operate the office equipment available, as it is not reasonable to assume that every office worker, however well trained, can instantly cope with every type and make of machine.

All of the above is known as *induction training*. It can take place over several days or it can be condensed into half a morning, according to the importance which an employer attaches to it. Training does not necessarily end after induction. Some companies, particularly the larger ones, have in-company training schemes, or allow their employees time to attend day courses or sandwich courses at nearby further education centres, or send them off on management courses, sales courses or secretarial training courses for anything from a few days to several weeks. If you obtain a job at such a company you will be fortunate indeed, as your personal growth and career opportunities will be almost assured.

Companies with good training schemes usually also have a 'promotion-from-within' policy, which has great advantages not only for the employer, but also for the able and ambitious employee. In order to help them to promote capable employees, many companies carry out an appraisal of each employee, once a year or more often. Using a standard form or 'merit-rating card', every department head rates each of his subordinates for punctuality, cooperation, leadership, and so on, using a scale from 1 to 5 or from A to E, that is, from 'excellent' to 'poor'.

Some companies believe in discussing the appraisal with the employee concerned, while others simply send the assessment to the employee and ask him or her to sign the form and return it

These assessments are designed to help an employer not only with his promotion-from-within policy, but also to compensate an employee adequately when pay increases are considered. Properly used, they can be extremely valuable, but can be unpopular, however, both with employees and with those called upon to make the assessments.

## The personnel department

As we saw earlier in this chapter, the personnel function can be carried out by any one of a number of different people, depending on the size of the company. In the larger companies there is a personnel department, sometimes with a personnel director at its head, for the really successful company realises that its greatest asset can be its workforce.

Apart from recruiting, selecting and supervising the training of staff, the personnel department has the following responsibilities:

**Salary administration**

A company which wants to attract and keep worthwhile employees must establish an equitable wage and salary policy, and offer fringe benefits comparable to those offered by other companies of the same size and type. Then a wage and salary structure must be set, so that every company employee knows where he or she is going or what the opportunities are, given the necessary effort. There are salary reviews to negotiate, pension schemes to work out and administer, and sometimes company insurance schemes, profit-sharing plans and other fringe benefits.

**Comfort, health and safety**

It is an employer's responsibility to provide his employees with a safe and healthy environment in which to work. There are several laws which cover these aspects of work, which are dealt with in the next chapter, and it is mainly the personnel department's responsibility to see that these regulations are complied with. Employees also have to play their part to make sure they are not injured while at work. They should follow safety instructions where they exist, make sure electricity cables are not left trailing along the floor, close drawers after use, be aware of the fact that you cannot open all the drawers in a filing cabinet without it toppling over, and take all other sensible precautions against accident as they would at home.

**Services and recreation**
Employee services often include a canteen, and almost always refreshment machines, or the traditional 'tea lady', all of which have to be planned and supervised. Also under this heading are social or sports clubs, as well as other recreational facilities, suggestion schemes, employee counselling, and such considerate activities as visiting sick employees, whether at home or in hospital, and making sure they are being looked after.

**Communications and consultation**
Keeping the staff informed is one of the most vital functions of the personnel department, accompanied by maintaining liaison with the elected union representatives and consulting them where necessary. This function is often carried out by means of company newsletters or magazines, as well as via bulletin boards, memos, staff meetings and informal talks.

**Staff records**
It goes without saying that the personnel department also keeps staff records. These usually consist of a file for each employee containing his or her original application form and resulting correspondence, the first position offered and the subsequent history of promotions, rises in salary, training, health and attendance record, and relevant outside activities, for instance lectures given, papers delivered to learned societies, books published, and so on. Sometimes the main points are summarised on index cards for easy access and to enable statistics to be collated without undue searching. Staff records are, of course, confidential, and those who keep them should make quite sure they are under lock and key at all times when not in use.

**Questions**
1 Your employer is about to start a recruitment campaign for staff. List four sources of manpower which he could tap.
2 You are seeking secretarial employment. List four ways in which you could go about it.
3 What are the advantages and disadvantages of speculative applications?
4 Describe items you would expect to see covered in a typical contract of employment for an office worker.    (LCC PSC Office Organisation and Secretarial Procedures)
5 You are secretary to a busy executive and because of an increasing work load you are to have an assistant. How can you help her to become useful in her job, as quickly as possible, without having to disrupt your own work unduly at peak times in order to explain and instruct?    (LCC PSC Office Organisation and Secretarial Procedures)
6 Describe items and information you think it would be useful to include in a day's induction course for a new receptionist to enable her to perform the work efficiently as soon as possible. (LCC PSC Office Organisation and Secretarial Procedures)
7 Your company has inserted the following advertisement in a newspaper:
    SENIOR SECRETARY required for busy sales office. The applicant should be over 25 with experience in a similar post. For further details, telephone 01-111-1234, extension 84.

Describe the preparations that you consider should be made by the member of staff on extension 84.    (LCC PSC Office Organisation and Secretarial Procedures)

# 16

# Work and the Law

Any person or company employing workers has to comply with several rules and regulations. These are incorporated in a number of laws which can be divided into two groups: those covering employment proper, and those covering health and safety at work. A brief summary of the main provisions is given below.

## Employment legislation

**Equal Pay Act 1970** (as amended by the *Employment Protection Act 1975* and the *Sex Discrimination Act 1975*)   This Act stipulates that an individual woman is entitled to equal treatment with a man with regard to pay, and other terms of her contract of employment, when employed on the same or broadly similar work to that of the man, or on work which though different is given an equal value under job evaluation. An employer can only avoid this one if he can show that any variation in treatment is due to a real difference, such as qualifications or length of service, between the two employees.

**Employment Agencies Act 1973** (as amended by the *Employment Protection Act 1975*)   This Act regulates the running of employment agencies and employment businesses. The latter employ their own workers and hire them out to work for others. One of the main stipulations of the Act is that agencies may not charge a fee for finding a worker a job. This is a good point to bear in mind if you decide to try an agency when seeking employment.

**Rehabilitation of Offenders Act 1974** This Act aims at shielding the offender with only one conviction from being pursued by prejudice. If a person convicted of certain offences keeps to the straight and narrow for a certain period, the conviction becomes spent and cannot be given as proper grounds for dismissal from employment, or for prejudicial treatment on the job. However, certain occupations and professions are excluded from these provisions.

**Trade Union and Labour Relations Acts 1974 and 1976** The provisions of these Acts come under three main headings: (1) the status and regulation of trade unions and employers' associations; (2) trade unions and the law, which covers the right to strike, to picket, and similar matters; (3) the Press charter, which deals with freedom of the press and allied matters.

**Employment Protection Act 1975** Most of the provisions of this Act have been consolidated into the *Employment Protection (Consolidation) Act 1978*, which we shall consider later. The main provisions still covered by this Act deal with collective bargaining, and consultation with unions when redundancies are under consideration.

**Sex Discrimination Act 1975** This Act makes it unlawful to discriminate between the sexes in employment, education, training and in the provision of housing, goods, facilities, and services to the public. In the employment field, it is also unlawful to discriminate against married couples. Moreover, an employer may not discriminate between the sexes when offering chances of promotion, training, transfer, or other facilities and benefits, and when dismissing employees.

The Act does not apply to small firms with five employees or less, nor to private households. There are other exceptions, for example when a man and a woman are obviously not interchangeable, as perhaps in the acting profession. Single-sex institutions are likewise excepted.

Discrimination between the sexes is also barred from most job advertisements, which have to make it clear that the openings are for either sex.

**Race Relations Act 1976** This Act is similar to the *Sex Discrimination Act*, and makes it unlawful to discriminate on grounds of colour, race, nationality, or ethnic or national origin, in employment, training, education, housing and the provision of goods, facilities and services. As far as employment is concerned, the Act covers both the recruitment of workers and the treatment of those already on the payroll. Private households are excluded from the provisions of this Act also and there are other exceptions, such as, for instance, where belonging to a particular ethnic group is a genuine requirement for a job.

**Employment Protection (Consolidation) Act 1978**   This Act brings together, or consolidates, the provisions on employment rights previously contained in the *Redundancy Payments Acts 1965 and 1969*, the *Contracts of Employment Act 1972*, the *Trade Union and Labour Relations Acts 1974 and 1976*, and the *Employment Protection Act 1975*. Its provisions cover redundancy payments, contracts of employment, and general protection for employees.

Redundancy payments are non-taxable lump sums paid to employees who become redundant after 104 weeks of continuous service with the same employer. The amount payable depends on the employee's age, length of service and salary.

By definition, a contract of employment exists as soon as the employee starts work, thereby demonstrating his or her acceptance of its terms and conditions. It can be an oral contract, and the employer is under no legal obligation to provide a written contract, except in the case of apprentices.

As we saw in the previous chapter, however, an employer must give every employee a written statement of particulars of the main terms of employment within thirteen weeks of starting work. Such details will include job title, pay, hours, holiday and holiday pay, sick leave and sick pay, pension and notice. Details of disciplinary rules and the grievance procedure must also be included.

The main provisions under the heading of general protection for employees cover guaranteed pay of up to five days a quarter for employees either laid off or on short time; guaranteed pay for up to twenty-six weeks for employees absent for medical reasons; maternity pay and reinstatement in her job for the pregnant employee; the right to join or not to join a trade union without being victimised; time off to attend union meetings or some public duties such as local authority meetings; the right to receive an itemised statement setting out gross pay, deductions, and net pay, or a summary of fixed deductions provided they are explained in an annual statement; and the right to a written statement of reasons for dismissal, and the right not to be unfairly dismissed.

**Employment Acts 1980 and 1982**   These Acts aim to restrict the power of trade unions to put pressure on individuals and employers, while enjoying immunity from the law when organising strikes and other industrial action. The Acts deal with secondary picketing, the closed shop, the right of an employer to compete for commercial contracts without union pressure, and several other matters. The regulation of the closed shop is by no means complete as yet, and further codes of practice can be expected on this issue.

## Health and safety legislation

**Employers' Liability (Compulsory Insurance) Act 1969**   This Act obliges employers to take out insurance against liability for bodily injury or disease sustained by their employees while employed in Great Britain. Nationalised industries, local authorities and police authorities are exempted from this provision.

**Offices, Shops and Railway Premises Act 1963**   This is one of the two main Acts concerned with health and safety in the office. Its provisions in some respects are modest indeed and have generally been exceeded by the best employers. They consist of the following:

(*a*)   Premises, furniture and fittings must be kept clean.
(*b*)   Rooms must be ventilated, 'suitably and sufficiently' lit and have a reasonable working temperature. The Act does not specify what is reasonable ventilation and lighting, but a temperature of less than 16°C after the first hour is not deemed to be reasonable.
(*c*)   Each worker must be allotted a space of at least 3·7 square metres or, if the ceiling is lower than three metres, then 11 cubic metres.
(*d*)   Suitable and sufficient lavatories must be provided and they must be properly maintained and easily accessible.
(*e*)   Washing facilities, with hot and cold water, soap, towels or other drying facilities must be provided.

(*f*)    Drinking water must be available.

(*g*)    Provisions must be made for keeping and drying clothes not used at work.

(*h*)    Sedentary workers must be provided with seating suitably designed for their work, and other workers must have access to seating.

(*i*)    Floors, passages and stairs must be safe and free from obstruction and substances likely to cause a person to slip.

(*j*)    Machinery must have dangerous parts fenced or be placed so that there is no risk of injury to employees.

(*k*)    No worker should be required to carry, lift or move a load heavy enough to cause injury.

(*l*)    One or more first-aid boxes or cupboards must be maintained, according to the number of employees. The person or persons put in charge of the first-aid boxes must be suitably trained and first-aid and accident procedure must be made known to all employees. A first-aid room may be provided instead of a box or cupboard.

A few further provisions are more relevant to shops than offices and there is a long section on fire precautions. The fire sections in this Act, together with those in the *Factories Act* were repealed in 1977, and replaced by Orders giving fire authorities the prime responsibility for general fire precautions in premises subject to these two Acts.

**Health and Safety at Work Act 1974**    This is an Act in which everyone is expected to participate: employers, the self-employed, employees, as well as designers, manufacturers, importers and suppliers of articles and substances for use at work. Each of these groups is meant to contribute in its own way to health and safety at work.

This Act is an addition to the existing health and safety legislation, such as the *Offices, Shops and Railway Premises Act 1963*, the main provisions of which remain in force until repealed and replaced by new regulations.

One of the main objectives of the Act is to involve both management and workers, so that all are made aware of the importance of achieving high standards of health and safety.

The aims of the Act are fourfold: (*a*) to secure the health, safety and welfare of persons at work; (*b*) to protect the health and safety of the general public from potentially harmful activities: (*c*) to control the keeping and use of explosive or highly flammable or otherwise dangerous substances, and to prevent the unlawful acquisition, possession and use of such substances; (*d*) to control the emission into the atmosphere of harmful or offensive substances from work premises.

## Duties of the employer

The employer must provide his employees with:

1 A safe place of work with a safe entrance and exit;
2 Safe equipment, efficiently maintained;
3 Safe work systems;
4 A safe working environment and adequate facilities for their welfare;
5 Safe methods of handling, storing and transporting goods;
6 Instruction, training and supervision of safe practices;
7 Consultation on making and maintaining health and safety arrangements and promoting them;
8 If he has five or more employees, he must also provide a written statement of his general policy on health and safety at work and arrangements in force for carrying it out.

An employer has the further duty of protecting the public, customers, delivery men and any other visitor to the premises.

## Duties of the employee

It is the duty of every employee, including the management, to:

1 Take reasonable care of his own health and safety while at work, and of the health and safety of others with whom he comes in contact;
2 Cooperate with the employer in fulfilling his obligations under the Act;
3 Refrain from misusing or interfering with anything provided for his health, safety or welfare.

## Duties of manufacturers and suppliers of articles and substances for use at work

Designers, manufacturers and suppliers must, as appropriate:

1   Design, manufacture and supply plant, machinery, equipment, components or substances which are safe and have been properly tested and examined;
2   Make available information on the correct use of the article or substance;
3   Carry out research to eliminate or minimise the risks to health and safety of the article or substance.

### How you can help

You will have gathered from the above that it is not merely commonsense that should induce you, as an employee, to look after your own health and safety, but that you are legally obligated to do so. Elsewhere in this book we have mentioned dangers of which you should be aware, and precautions you should take, and here are a few more:

1   Follow instructions when using machinery. Do not take 'short cuts'. When the task is done, switch off the machine and remove the plug by taking hold of it, *not* by pulling the cord.
2   If a machine is not working properly or is out of order, report it or call a mechanic yourself, according to company custom. On no account tamper with the machine yourself.
3   Make sure that dangerous machines are fitted with guards and report any irregularity such as fraying flexes.
4   Bear in mind that long hair and dangling jewellery can get caught in machines and proceed accordingly.
5   Keep containers of typewriter correcting and cleaning fluids closed when not in use, as many of them give off highly flammable vapours and some of them cause headaches, as you may have noticed.
6   Never stand on a swivel chair for any reason. It is very dangerous.
7   Comply with notices relating to safety regulations in general and fire precautions in particular.

Once you become conscious of the need for safety, acting in such a way as to ensure your own safety and that of those around you will become second nature.

**Questions**

1  Briefly describe the main provisions of any three Acts of Parliament which particularly affect the work of personnel departments in relation to staff recruitment, appointment, dismissal and working conditions.      (LCC PSC Office Organisation and Secretarial Procedures)

2  The *Health and Safety at Work Act, 1974* requires the participation of employees as well as employers. What would you, as an employee, have to do to fulfil the requirements of this Act?

3  Give examples of some employers who are exempted from the provisions of the Sex Discrimination Act 1975.

4  What are the fourfold aims of the *Health and Safety at Work Act, 1974*?

5  List four ways in which you can contribute to the safety of your office as a working environment.

# Appendix

# Sources of Information

There will be times when you will feel that your employer expects
you to know the answer to all questions. This can be rather
unnerving until you realise that all you really need to know is where
to go to find the answers.

A list of reference books is given below. This does not mean that
you will need all of them either on your desk or in your office. For
one thing, needs vary according to the type of business, or according
to preference and personal taste. Furthermore, all these reference
books, or most of them, will be available at your local reference
library, and that is the first place you should turn to, not only if you
need to find out the answer to one specific question, but also if your
chief should ask you to carry out a piece of more extensive research.

The yellow pages of the telephone directory are another source of
useful information if you should need to know the names and
addresses of suppliers of goods and services of all sorts, including
interpreters, translators, and employment agencies. For all matters
concerned with trade, get in touch with your local chamber of
commerce and industry, or with the Department of Trade and
Industry in London. Copies of Government publications are on sale at
Her Majesty's Stationery Office, PO Box 569, Stamford Street,
London SE1 9NY, or from one of the local offices.

Here are some useful reference books:

## General reference

*Directory of British Associations*   Gives the names and addresses
of professional associations, societies, research organisations,
chambers of trade and industry, and trade unions. It also indicates their activities and lists their publications.

*Guide to British Enterprise* (Dun & Bradstreet)   Lists names and registered addresses of companies, as well as their subsidiaries or parent companies, and their fields of activity.

*Hansard*   This is the official, word-for-word report of proceedings in Parliament. You will find it useful if you need to follow a particular debate or Bill on behalf of your chief.

*International Year Book and Statemen's Who's Who*   Gives facts and figures on every country in the world and biographical details of thousands of leading figures all over the world.

*Kelly's Post Office London Directory*   Lists businesses in the London postal area in alphabetical and street order, as well as classified into trades and professions. There are also several pages of street maps in full colour.

*Kelly's Manufacturers & Merchants Directory*   Lists alphabetically the names, addresses, telephone and Telex numbers of UK manufacturers, wholesalers and companies offering services to industry. There is also a classification into trade headings.

*UK Kompass Management Register*   This work is published in seven regional volumes and lists the leading industrial companies, with detailed information on each of them.

*UK Kompass Register*   A two-volume work listing names and addresses of suppliers of individual products and services. The first volume is classified by product, and the second is alphabetical. Other Kompass directories are available for most European countries.

*Municipal Year Book and Public Services Directory*   Gives information about local authorities in England and Wales. Each county council and district council is listed, together with areas, population, rates and names of chief officers.

*Pears Cyclopaedia*   This compact encyclopaedia gives a vast amount of information on many subjects. From the secretary's point of view perhaps the most useful sections are those on English law, the background to economic events, the world of science, and general information. The gazetteer of the world and the atlases can also be useful.

*Post Office Guide*   This volume contains everything you need to know about the postal services. It is published annually at a very modest price, and supplements are issued as required during the year.

*Stock Exchange Year Book*   Gives details of companies quoted on the Stock Exchange: registered address, capital, directors, and so on.

*Whitaker's Almanack*   A mine of information on just about everything: statistics on population, divorce and crime; British and world affairs for the past year, dates and data for the year ahead; names of Nobel prize winners; weights and measures; order of precedence. This last is invaluable when organising an event involving a number of distinguished people with honours, decorations, or titles and needing to seat them in the correct order.

*Who's Who*   This gives biographical information on prominent people in all fields of endeavour. There is also a *Who Was Who*; a *Who Owns Whom*, very useful in trying to sort out companies and their subsidiaries; and a number of specialist books, such as *Who's Who in the Theatre*. Similar volumes are available in France and the USA.

## Correct English

First and foremost, you need a good dictionary. Indeed, some experts would maintain that a dictionary is the *only* tool needed by anyone aspiring to write good English. Obviously, if you are dealing with technical, legal, medical or other highly specialised subjects, you will add the corresponding specialised dictionary or glossary of terms.

If you are working in a foreign language, of course you will need the appropriate dictionary for the language. It pays to select language dictionaries carefully, as they are by no means equally good. Moreover, some of them are geared more to the holiday visitor than to business.

Other aids to better writing are *Fowler's Modern English Usage* for help with fine points of grammar or correct usage, and *Roget's Thesaurus of English Words and Phrases*, a collection of synonyms, classified according to meaning, rather than alphabetically.

## Forms of Address

It is as well to bear in mind that the experts on forms of address do not all agree on every single point. It is therefore advisable to use one guide and stick to that. The acknowledged experts are the following:

*Titles and Forms of Address, A Guide to their Correct Use* (A. & C. Black)

*Debrett's Correct Forms*
*Debrett's Handbook, Distinguished People in British Life*
*Kelly's Handbook*, which also covers the titled, landed and official
  classes.
*Crockford's Directory*, which gives forms of address for clergymen
  in the Church of England.

# Travel

*AA* and *RAC Handbooks* give motoring information, distances
between towns, early closing days, breakdown services, hotels and
maps. For other forms of travel consult the following: *ABC Air/Rail
Europe and Middle East Guide, ABC Rail Guide, ABC Shipping
Guide, ABC World Airways Guide* and *Cook's Continental
Timetable*.

# Hotels and Restaurants

As we saw in Chapter 10, the *ABC Rail Guide* lists recommended
hotels throughout Britain, with details of special facilities they may
offer for executives. The following each have their own particular
slant:

*Hotels and Restaurants* is the official guide of the British Tourist
  Authority.
*The Financial Times World Hotel Directory* is aimed at the business
  traveller.
*Egon Ronay's TWA Guide to Good Restaurants in Europe's Busi-
  ness Cities* covers thirty-five cities in eighteen countries, and is
  especially written for the business traveller.
*Egon Ronay's Lucas Guide* is a hotel and restaurant guide and is
  useful for compiling a list of good places to which clients and
  prospective clients can be taken.
*The Good Food Guide* serves almost exactly the same purpose as
  the above.
*Michelin Guide* is a guide to Great Britain and Ireland, one in a
  series of famous and prestigious guides published in France. It
  lists both hotels and restaurants, and grades each according to
  very exacting standards. Restaurants are awarded one or more
  rosettes according to excellence, and restaurants all over the
  world vie for the privilege of being accorded a rosette by
  Michelin. Very few establishments get two or three. If you select

a Michelin-recommended restaurant you cannot go very far wrong, but your pocket, or more usually your company's pocket, has to be well-lined.

## Viewdata

As we have seen in several chapters of this book, information can be obtained not merely through books and periodicals, but also through the medium of the television screen. This type of communication is known variously as videotex, teletext and viewdata, which can be confusing, but according to British Telecom the term 'videotex' is most widely used internationally, while 'viewdata' is the common term in the UK.

There are both public and private viewdata services. As we saw in Chapter 5, one of the public services is called Ceefax and is provided by the BBC. Another is called Oracle and is provided by ITV. Both of these services are provided free of charge via the television screen. The type of information they supply covers weather and driving conditions, train timetables, plane arrivals and departures, and entertainment.

The third public viewdata service is Prestel, provided by British Telecom. We saw in Chapter 5 how it works. Every Prestel user has an official directory comprising a subject index, a company index, which is a list of companies on which Prestel provides information, a country index, which lists the countries on which information is provided, and a list of information providers. Alongside each listing is a code enabling the user to key directly into the information required, without having to go through all the stages of studying the index and so on. The information provided by Prestel ranges very widely indeed and is specifically geared to the business world. It is therefore the type of service you are most likely to find in an office.

Several makes of private viewdata systems are also available. Most of them form part of integrated office systems, as we saw in Chapter 14. Such services are recommended mainly for companies wishing to make maximum use of their own data. A multinational company, for instance, would be able to gain instant access to information stored at any of its subsidiaries in any part of the world.

If you own a word processor you do not even need a television screen, but can receive data via the VDU. Another interesting development is the NatWest Network. It enables customers of the National Westminster Bank in the United Kingdom or abroad to obtain an instant readout of their cash position, as well as other financial details, simply by touching a few buttons connected to a desk-top computer terminal. Finally, there is now also a Teleputer System, which, as the word implies, is a combined personal computer and videotex.

There is no doubt that in the near future *all* information stored by computer anywhere in the world will become available to any viewdata user anywhere on the globe. The only remaining problems then will be the protection of privacy and how to sift through it all to reach the piece of information required.

# Index

franking machines, 41–3, 44
Freefone, 103
Freepost, 48

Graphmate, 35
graphs, 30, 32–5

hardware *see* CPU
health and safety, 207–8
  legislation, 213–15, 216
hotel and restaurant guides, 131,
  222–3
house style, 22, 58
hyphen, 62

incoming mail, 37
indexes, 99, 142, 155–7
information, communication of,
  8, Chapters 5 and 7 *passim*
ink duplicating, 181–3
input peripherals, 197
inserters, 44
Integrated Services Digital
  Network (ISDN), 96
Intelpost, 47
interviews, 202, 205
invitations, 78–80
invoices, 9–10
ISO paper sizes, 87–8
itineraries, 132–6

journalists, dealing with, 111–12

lateral filing, 147, 149
letters, *see* business letters
letters of credit, 9, 164
line graphs, 30–4
loaning out a file, 152
loudspeaker phones, 97

mail, handling, 18, 28, 37–50
mailing equipment, 43–4
manager, 5, 7
meetings, formal, 114–21
  agenda, 115–17
  minutes, 121–2
  notice of meeting, 115

procedure, 118–19
  terms used, 120
meetings, informal, 121–4
memoranda, internal, 8, 74–5
Memorandum and Articles of
  Association, 2
MICR (Magnetic Ink Character
  Readers), 197
microfilm, 147–8
minutes, 120, 122
motions (in meetings), 118
multi-set forms, 11–13, 18, 89–90

National Giro, 162
National Insurance, 175
NCR paper, 90
notice of meeting, 115

OCR (Optical Character
  Reader), 189, 197–8
office
  design, 12, 17
  equipment, 187–99
  furniture, 14
  open plan, 13, 17
Offices, Shops and Railway
  Premises Act 1963, 17,
  213–14
offset-lithography, 182–3
open cheques, 166–7
Oracle, 82, 223
Orator (telephone service), 103
orders, 9
organisation charts, 5–8
organising and planning, 26–36
outgoing mail, 39–44
output peripherals, 198
overdrafts, 172
overseas telephone calls, 100

packing list, 9
paging systems, 8, 97
paper
  grades, 88–9
  sizes, 87–8
parcel post, 48–9
partnerships, 1–2